D1566941

EAST ASIAN HISTORICAL MONOGRAPHS
General Editor: WANG GUNGWU

CHINESE SOCIETY IN NINETEENTH CENTURY SINGAPORE

CHINESE SOCIETY IN NINETEENTH CENTURY SINGAPORE

LEE POH PING

1478
1978

KUALA LUMPUR
OXFORD UNIVERSITY PRESS
OXFORD NEW YORK MELBOURNE
1978

Oxford University Press
OXFORD LONDON GLASGOW
NEW YORK TORONTO MELCOURNE WELLINGTON
IBADAN NAIROBI DAR ES SALAAM CAPE TOWN
KUALA LUMPUR SINGAPORE JAKARTA HONG KONG TOKYO
DELHI BOMBAY CALCUTTA MADRAS KARACHI
 *Oxford University Press 1978*

ISBN 0 19 580384 1

*Printed in Singapore by Dainippon Tien Wah Printing (Pte) Ltd.
Published by Oxford University Press, 3 Jalan 13/3,
Petaling Jaya, Selangor, Malaysia*

CONTENTS

TABLES

MAPS

ACKNOWLEDGEMENT

MAPS 2, 3 and 4 are reprinted from G. W. Skinner's *Chinese Society in Thailand*. Copyright © 1957 by Cornell University. Used by permission of Cornell University Press.

PREFACE

THE phenomenon of chronic instability in Chinese society during the latter part of the nineteenth century was first brought to my attention by Benedict R. O. G. Andersen, the chairman of my committee when I was a student in the Government Department in Cornell University. He suggested that some attempt be made to explain this instability. Acting on his suggestion, I began to study the primary and secondary accounts of the innumerable riots that then rocked this society, and I emerged rather unsatisfied. The accounts seemed to overplay the religious, regional, and secret society divisions among the Chinese, while they totally ignored any contributory source from outside. Further research and thought soon convinced me that the real cause of the riots should not be sought in the divisions mentioned, but in British policy prior to intervention. It was in fact the British policy of free trade that created a new Chinese society which impinged on an older Chinese society then existing in Singapore, based on gambier and pepper agriculture. The inherent instability of the free trade society and its clash with the gambier and pepper society produced the social convulsions. These convulsions were not overcome until the British changed their policy from free trade to colonialism.

In pursuing this argument in this book which is a modified version of a doctoral thesis accepted by Cornell University in January 1974, I have been greatly aided by the basic research of Wong Lin Ken on the trade of Singapore and of Mary Turnbull on the history of the Straits Settlements, both dealing with topics around the same period.[1] The approach here is sociopolitical as I have essentially tried to show how political events and institutions, broadly defined, have been influenced by the social structure. Thus

---

1. Wong Lin Ken, 'The Trade of Singapore, 1819-69', *Journal of Royal Asiatic Society (Malayan Branch)*, Vol. XXXIII, No. 4 (1960). C. M. Turnbull, *The Straits Settlements 1826-67, Indian Presidency to Crown Colony* (London, The Athlone Press, 1972).

421

22121421222

the first chapter is devoted to the justification of such an approach. The adoption of such a method of analysis owes much to Barrington Moore who used it to explain the origins of dictatorship and democracy in six countries.[2]

The reader will find that Chinese societies in the other two states of the Straits Settlements, Penang and Malacca, are not included despite the fact that they were subject to a similar British policy and despite the existence of linkages between these two societies and the one in Singapore. The latter fact is however discussed whenever necessary but the justification in excluding the two states is that we are basically concerned with the effect of British policy on one society, that is, Singapore, and that, a diligent search notwithstanding, sufficient sources on them do not seem to exist to allow for reasonable treatment.

Many people have helped me in the preparation of this book. First of all I would like to acknowledge my debt to Benedict R. O. G. Andersen and Wang Gungwu, the former for suggesting this topic and for subsequently going through various drafts of my original thesis with a very fine comb, and the latter for very valuable suggestions regarding the structure of the book. David Mozingo, Eldon Kenworthy, T. J. Pempel, Don Horowitz, Hidehiro Okada, and Yen Ching Hwang have also offered suggestions at various stages in the preparation of both the thesis and the book. I need hardly say that they are in no way responsible for any errors of fact and judgement that may arise.

For help in the location of sources, particularly Chinese ones, I am grateful to Lee Yip Lim, Tan Yoek Seong, Kua Bak Lim, and Tan Ee Leong. For the financial support which sustained me in the pursuit of my degree in Cornell University, I would like to thank the Ford Foundation whose money was funnelled through the University of Malaya-University of Pittsburgh project. In this connexion, I would also like to thank George Kahin for initially making it possible for me to study in Cornell. Finally, I would like to thank my friends in 102, West Avenue, particularly A. C. Milner, Ray Ileto, Barbara Harvey, P. C. Hauswedell, Stanley Bedlington, Robert Taylor, Carl Trocki and Thak Chaloemtiarana, for many hours of companionship, frequently spent in prolonged lunches. The resulting conversations may not have contributed in

2. Barrington Moore, Jr., *Social Origins of Dictatorship and Democracy; Lord and Peasant in the making of the Modern World* (Boston, Beacon Press, 1967).

a material way to this book but they certainly sharpened my dialectical skills.

University of Malaya,   LEE POH PING
Kuala Lumpur,
July 1976

A NOTE ON THE SOURCES AND ROMANIZATION

A distressing aspect of research on Chinese society in nineteenth century Singapore is the lack of sources, particularly in Chinese. I am of the opinion that the suppression of the secret societies in 1890 and the Japanese Occupation were responsible for the destruction of much relevant material. Nevertheless, I believe that it is possible to construct a reasonable picture of this society from the material, Chinese and English, which remains. In most cases, however, I have attempted to reduce inferential statements to the minimum and to follow the text as closely as possible.

The romanization of Chinese names and terms, particularly of those found among the Chinese in South-East Asia, is always a problem. Strictly speaking, such romanization should follow the Mandarin pronunciation. But if this were done, it would render unfamiliar many famous names and institutions, traditionally romanized according to the pronunciation in their particular dialects. For example, the name of the overseas Chinese merchant, Tan Kah Kee (陳嘉庚), romanized according to the Hokkien pronunciation, would become Ch'en Chia Keng if romanized in Mandarin, while the internationally known Tan Tock Seng (陳篤生) Hospital would become Ch'en Tu Sheng Hospital. The solution adopted here is to follow the spellings of the names and terms in their respective dialects as they have appeared in historical records, official documents, newspapers, and other published works. In cases where they have not appeared, as far as I am able to discover, the romanization according to the Mandarin pronunciation is adopted.

I

THE JUSTIFICATION

THE socio-economic approach is desirable for several reasons,[1] among them it provides a more adequate explanation of the instability mentioned previously—an instability which was expressed in riots, the most serious of which were the secret society riots of 1854, 1857, and 1876, and the anti-Roman Catholic riot of 1851— than that provided by existing literature, which gives three different explanations.

One emphasizes the religious factor.[2] It argues that the basic reason for the riot of 1851 was the success of the Roman Catholic missionaries in winning converts among the Chinese. The consequence of such a conversion was that, if it did not reduce the ranks of the secret societies, it at least reduced the pool of Chinese from which the secret societies could draw their membership. Thus the secret societies had to attack the Catholics in order to prevent this competition from undermining their position.

While this may be valid, it can only be a partial explanation, simply because the missionaries had been successful in making converts both before and after 1851.[3] Why did anti-Catholic sentiment not erupt earlier? Nor does it explain why there was a strike of non-Christian workers on the gambier plantations and why there happened to be a disproportionate number of rich planters among the Catholics who were attacked.[4] There must have been a socio-economic basis. Those who argue this position tend not to look beyond that provided by the first newspaper accounts of the riot.[5] Where they do, their analysis is most contrived.[6] It will be shown that the basic reason for the riot was the attempt by the free traders to remove planters and workers from their plantations, and put new settlers, many of them Catholics, in their place. The aggrieved planters and workers then made use of the secret societies to attack the Catholics.

The second approach sees the cause of instability as conflict among the major dialect groups, of which there were five in Singapore at that time. 'Dialect group' refers to a group of Chinese who speak a particular dialect and originate from a particular territory in China. (See Chapter III.) The 1854 and 1876 riots particularly are interpreted as resulting from rivalry between the two larger dialect groups, the Hokkiens and the Teochews.[7] There is some truth in this view.[8] But it fails through its inability to explain satisfactorily the rivalry between the two groups, attributing it to some innate quarrelsomeness of the Chinese or to a rivalry in China of which the Singapore conflict was only an extension.[9] In other words, the economic basis of the conflict is not stressed. This book, on the other hand, will show that the basic cause of the two riots was the attempt by the free traders to wrest from the Teochews their rice and remittance business, the Hokkiens here being used as bridgeheads.

The third approach is the most pervasive. It sees the underlying cause of the major riots and other lesser ones in the latter half of the nineteenth century as activities of the secret societies. Some writers, accordingly, view the 1854 riot simply as the product of secret society rivalry.[10] Others believe the 1854 and 1876 riots and the many attempts by the secret societies to obstruct the prosecution of justice to have been instigated by people intent on using the societies to create an *imperium in imperio* in Singapore.[11] Still others ascribe the many crimes committed in that period to the secret societies which were presumed to be basically criminal in nature.[12]

This third approach demonstrates a certain richness and variety in the linkages drawn between the secret societies and the social convulsions of the time. What is surprising, however, is that this literature fails to examine either the social convulsions or the secret societies within the socio-economic context. It will be argued that the reason why the secret societies were so pervasive was that their violent methods and emphasis on ritual solidarity were peculiarly suited to a population living in a pioneer economy, which was tough and not generally settled in the sense that there were few families.

We must also give some consideration to the nature of imperialism. One of the theoretical problems in the study of imperialism has been to understand how apparently conflicting forces within the imperial society cohere in their impingement on an alien society. For example, one force, the government of the metropolitan society, may see a colony primarily in strategic or even 'civilizing' terms.

Such an attitude may not be wholly congruent with that of another force, the industrial and financial elements in the metropolitan society whose aims are presumed to be wholly exploitative.[13] There is also a specific variant of this problem in our case. The literature on Singapore before the 1870s makes great play with the difference in attitudes of the European mercantile community there and the government in India, which ruled Singapore up to 1867, as to how it should be run. The latter saw it merely as a trading station which would facilitate the protection of shipping to China through the Straits of Malacca, while the former saw it primarily as a base for free trade. In their view, nothing should be done to hamper this trade or the free supply of labour, and certainly no taxes should be imposed beyond the barest essentials.[14]

While this book makes no claim to contribute substantially to the theoretical literature on imperialism, it does argue that in our case there was no real problem either on a general or a specific level. As far as the imperialism of free trade is concerned, there was no conflict between strategic and commercial considerations. Commerce, or free trade in this case, could not be effectively conducted until there was some reasonable protection for the shipping routes along which the ships sailed, carrying manufactured goods from Britain and raw produce to it. As Robinson and Gallagher have pointed out, all that was needed, under free trade, was to control small areas, strategically situated on the shipping routes, which could serve as bases for the protection of shipping and for the exchange of goods.[15] Singapore and Hongkong were two of the bases so created.

Specifically with regard to Singapore, when the government and the free traders moved in before the 1870s, they moved in as one. (Therefore these terms are used interchangeably in this book.) This can be seen from the fact that the most important functions of the government, taxation, and the management of land,[16] worked basically to the benefit of the free traders. Furthermore, the government drew the bulk of its revenue from the tax-farming of opium and gambling, for which the Chinese were the chief, if not the only, consumers. This coincided with the wishes of the free traders, for they were not against taxation in general, only against taxes on themselves. Though much play has been made with the unsuitability for Europeans of the land tenure system existing in Singapore before the 1830s this system survived mainly because of the indifference of the free traders.[17] There was no point in agitating for a changed system so long as the free traders saw no profit from commercial agriculture. But, when the British market lowered tariffs for Eastern produce from the 1830s onwards, the free traders evinced a new interest in investing in commercial agriculture in Singapore. It was then only a matter of time before the land tenure system was altered for their benefit, though great numbers of Chinese were evicted in the process.

The origins of the Chinese 'problem', much belaboured in the literature on the overseas Chinese in South-East Asia, must now be considered. This problem has been perceived, by those who identify with the nationalism of the South-East Asians, as the retention by the Chinese of their separate identity. Or, in other words, since the Chinese do not have one identity but many, the problem consists of the difficulty the Chinese pose for assimilation policies, whether Singaporean or some other South-East Asian identity.[18]

It is demonstrable that the origins of the problem, in Singapore at least, arose from socio-economic developments. Essentially, the present position of the Chinese originated in the free-trade period of British imperialism, and was consolidated by political colonialism. This imperialism began the process of placing the Chinese in the position of middlemen in an economy where the Europeans were above and the indigenous South-East Asians below. Thus was destroyed whatever independent economic existence the Chinese might have had or whatever assimilation of the Chinese into Malay society might have occurred. The functioning of the economy was such that the Europeans would not assimilate the Chinese, and because that functioning necessitated the presence of large numbers of Chinese in Singapore, the Chinese were able and encouraged to retain their Chinese identity.

In South-East Asia as a whole, the varying identities that many Chinese held after decolonization, such as that of the *peranakan* in Indonesia, the Chinese *mestizos* in the Philippines, and the assimilated Chinese in Thailand, resulted from the different colonial experience of these South-East Asian countries and, in the case of Thailand, the non-colonial experience. We shall elaborate this argument by considering the cultural explanation for assimilation, advanced by Skinner and Wickberg.

Skinner's main concern in an article comparing the Chinese in Java and Thailand is why the Chinese are more assimilated in Thailand than in Java. Skinner argues that the reason is that the

Chinese did not find Javanese culture, its prestige diminished by the colonial experience, attractive, and therefore did not adopt it. Since Thailand, however, was uncolonized, its culture did not prove unattractive to the Chinese. Consequently, many did adopt Thai ways.[19] Wickberg pursues this same line of reasoning for the Philippines where he argues that while it was not possible for a Chinese to become a Spaniard, nevertheless some Chinese accepted Filipino culture because much of it was Spanish. A Chinese *mestizo* group therefore grew up in the Philippines half-way in the assimilation continuum between the *peranakan* of Indonesia and the assimilated Chinese in Thailand.[20]

Skinner and Wickberg use a social anthropological approach. They incorporate elements of social structure and culture in their explanation of the phenomenon of assimilation. But such is their emphasis on the cultural aspect that it is elevated to the status of an independent variable. A culture was adopted essentially because it was attractive. It so happened that in Thailand and the Philippines, the local culture was attractive because it belonged to people high up in the socio-economic structure. The inference was that a culture could be attractive for other reasons and still be adopted by the Chinese.

A cultural explanation has, of course, some validity but, as Barrington Moore says, only if it is derivative, rather than independent, of the socio-economic explanation.[21] For culture changes with the times and men are moved not by ideas or any other cultural variable but by the struggle for existence. Successful Chinese adopted Thai culture not because it was intrinsically attractive but because it made easier the obtaining from the Thai *élite* the economic favours necessary to their prosperity, and the political protection needed to guard their property. There was, by contrast, very little of a material nature that the Chinese could gain from adopting Javanese culture during the colonial period. But when it became a matter of existence, when non-assimilation could pose a threat to future prospects or to property, many Chinese adopted Indonesian culture, as evinced by the extensive adoption of Indonesian names after the 1965 coup. One may also add that many Chinese adopted Cambodian culture during the colonial period when Cambodian culture was demeaned, essentially because there were economic reasons for doing so.[22] So much for the cultural argument.

A socio-economic approach seems likely to be more illuminating. It will first be considered why the Chinese were not given a place of political honour by the Europeans. The answer is that the Chinese lacked the economic power to force the Europeans to open their ranks.

If one considers the experience of the industrialized countries, particularly England, the United States, Germany, and Japan, the relevance of such an approach is clear. In the England of the enclosures and the United States of the Civil War, the commercial class proved so powerful that it could compel the landed class to alter the political system to one in their favour (a democratic system). In the Germany of the Junkers and the Japan of the Meiji, the commercial class was not strong enough. Nevertheless it was sufficient to compel the landed class to respect its power. The solution of the landed class to the challenge was partly assimilation. The point is that the ability of a commercial class to get what it wants is a function of the leverage it has on the economy. If in Germany and Japan the commercial class could not create democracy, it could at least partially enter the ruling class.

If the Chinese were unable to force the Europeans to assimilate them or, at least, to give them a place of political honour in South-East Asia, it was because they were much weaker than their German and Japanese counterparts. The primary reason for their weakness was the presence in South-East Asia of a rival European commercial class which dominated the colonial economy by fulfilling two vital functions.

First, in an international economic setting where the imperial countries manufactured goods and South-East Asia supplied the raw materials and minerals, this European commercial class provided the key linkage of exchange by its control of the local import and export sector, made possible by its system of agency houses and by the control of shipping. Second, it supplied much of the capital and high-level skill needed in the extraction of minerals and raw materials. As a consequence, the colonial economy could not function without it.

The Chinese basically were needed for two functions: to be the middlemen between the European upper commercial class and the indigenous people of South-East Asia, and to provide labour in the extraction of raw materials and minerals. (The latter need, however, was only significant in Malaya and Singapore.) But these functions did not allow the Chinese to exert much leverage on the colonial economy for, as middlemen, they were dependent on the Europeans for both capital and goods. Nor could they make much headway, even if they wanted to, in mobilizing the natives for leverage since they were separated from them by race. In Singapore and Malaya, despite the presence of a large labour force in the tin and rubber industries, the Chinese middlemen were still basically tied to the Europeans because the rubber and tin were used by them. Moreover, it was a system quite profitable to these middlemen, and hence there was no powerful incentive to mobilize this labour force against controllers of the colonial economy. Only with the depression of the 1930s, when prices for tin and rubber collapsed, did the Chinese merchants attempt to develop some autonomy by their investment outside the import and export sector. But the investment was not overwhelming and no fundamental independence was achieved.

In such a situation, except for the few who were permitted to absorb European culture, the Chinese had three choices, either to retain their Chinese identity, or to assimilate to the indigenous South-East Asian peoples, or to follow a course somewhere in between. What they ultimately chose was determined by the number of Chinese the colonial economy in each South-East Asian country needed and what possibility there was for carrying on an existence independent of the indigenous population. Mostly, but not always, this was determined by the proportion of the Chinese to the indigenous population in each particular South-East Asian country. The situation in all the colonized countries and Thailand, excepting Malaya and Singapore, was such that while in the colonial period the numbers of Chinese increased, they did not increase enough to re-sinify all the Chinese who had gone some way towards assimilation as the existence of the Chinese *mestizos* in the Philippines and the *peranakan* in Indonesia in significant numbers would testify.

But re-sinification went a long way in Malaya and Singapore, because the colonial economy allowed for the migration of great numbers of Chinese (in Malaya they constituted nearly half of the total population, while in Singapore they comprised about three-quarters). Moreover, they were to a great extent self-sufficient within this economy. By this is meant that they obtained their livelihood fairly independently of the Malay population in Malaya. Save for the middleman economic role they played between the Europeans and the Malays, the Chinese lived essentially by themselves, dependent only on the Europeans because of the European control of the import and export sector and of the police. This was particularly so in the case of Singapore where the bulk of them were involved in service occupations derived from the efforts of other Chinese elsewhere in South-East Asia.[23] Even those who were partially assimilated, like the Malacca Chinese, had to re-sinify to some extent in order to prosper. Thus many Chinese maintained their identity when the colonial power departed and were to pose a problem to the development of a Singaporean or Malaysian identity.

1. Because this is an exercise in social and political analysis, the Malay and Indian societies in Singapore will not be included, though the author is aware that Singapore, especially from the late nineteenth century onwards, played an important role in the dissemination of modern influences in the Malay world. See William Roff, 'The Malayo-Muslim World of Singapore at the Close of the Nineteenth Century', in *Journal of Asian Studies*, Vol. XXIV, No. 1 (November 1964), p.75.

2. See *Straits Times*, 4 March 1851; C. B. Buckley, *An Anecdotal History of Singapore in Old Times*, 1902 (Singapore, University of Malaya Press, 1965 reprint), p.543; Song Ong Siang, *One Hundred Years of the Chinese in Singapore*, 1923 (Singapore, University of Malaya Press, 1967 reprint), pp.83 and 161; Leon Comber, *Chinese Secret Societies in Malaya, a Survey of the Triad Society from 1800 to 1900* (New York, Locust Valley, A.A.S., 1969), p.77; Wilfred Blythe, *The Impact of Secret Societies in Malaya* (London, Oxford University Press, 1969), pp.70-1.

3. See *Singapore Free Press*, 27 July 1849, and J. D. Vaughan, *Manners and Customs of the Chinese in the Straits Settlements* (Singapore, Mission Press, 1879), p.15.

4. See J. F. A. McNair, *Prisoners their own Warders* (London, A. Constable, 1899), p.68; Comber, op. cit., p.79.

5. The *Straits Times*, 4 March 1851.

6. See Chapter IV.

7. See Vaughan, op. cit., p.95; Song, op. cit., p.87; Buckley, op. cit., p.585; Blythe, op. cit. (to some extent), p.76; J. Cameron, *Our Tropical Possessions in Malayan India, being a Descriptive Account of Singapore, Penang, Province Wellesley, and Malacca; their Peoples, Products, Commerce and Government* (London, Smith Elder and Co., 1865), p.265; C. M. Turnbull, *The Straits Settlements 1826-67, Indian Presidency to Crown Colony* (London, University of London, Athlone Press, 1972), p.115; the Petition of the Ghee Hin (a major secret society) in the *Singapore Free Press*, 18 February 1889. See also P'an Hsing-nung, *Ma-la-ya ch'ao-ch'iao t'ung-chien (The Teochews in Malaya)*, Singapore, 1950.

8. Most of the sources quoted in footnote 7 see it as rivalry between the two dialect groups; those who see it strictly as a secret society affair (see footnote 10) tend to be in a minority.

9. For example, Buckley, op. cit., p.585, states that 'a quarrel arose between the Hokkiens and the Teochews because the former refused to join in a subscription to assist the rebels who had been driven from Amoy by the Chinese Imperial Troops'. Blythe, op. cit., p.76, also states that there was 'in China, a long-standing feud between Tiechius and Hokkiens, of which this quarrel was undoubtedly a further manifestation'.

10. Comber, op. cit., p.82; W. H. Read, *Play and Politics* (London, Weels and Co., 1901), p.92.

11. *Singapore Free Press*, 8 January 1857; the Governor of the Straits Settlements quoted in Blythe, op. cit., pp.89-90; Comber, op. cit., p.96, for the 1857 riot. See Song Ong Siang, op. cit., p.85; Read, op. cit., for the 1876 riot. For the *imperium in*

imperio literature, see L. A. Mills, *British Malaya, 1824-1867* (Singapore, Oxford University Press reprint, 1966), p.213; W. A. Pickering, 'Chinese in the Straits of Malacca', *Fraser's Magazine* (bound) (London, Longmans and Green, October 1876), p.439; James Jackson, *Planters and Speculators, Chinese and European Agricultural Enterprise in Malaya 1786-1921* (Singapore, University of Malaya Press, 1968), p.3.

12. For some suggestion of this from a Chinese source, see Li Chung-chio, *Hsin-chia-po feng t'u chi (A Description of Singapore)*, Singapore, 1947. For other examples in English sources, see *Singapore Free Press*, 9 March 1865; 26 February 1849; *Straits Settlements Secret Correspondence* 'R. F. Wingrove to Murchison', 23 July 1830; *Singapore Chronicle*, 3 March 1831.

13. One of the arguments put forward by those who defend imperialism is that the metropolitan countries did not gain economically from the colonies; rather the colonies proved to be white elephants. The indicator they use is the marginal nature of the total British investment in the colonies. For an example, see D. K. Fieldhouse, 'Imperialism: An Historiographical Revision', *The Economic History Review*, Second Series XIV, No. 2 (1961), pp.187-209. Presumably then, Britain acquired her colonies for other than economic reasons. But, as D. R. Sardesai in 'Trade and Empire in Malaya and Singapore, 1869-1874' (Athens, Ohio, 1970) points out, there were economic considerations other than investment. He quotes Albert H. Imlah, *Economic Elements in the Pax Britannica* (Cambridge, Mass., Harvard University Press, 1958) as writing that the chronic deficit in British visible trade in the nineteenth century was made up by so-called invisible exports like shipping, insurance, and banking. Moreover, there was profit from trade.

14. This is found or suggested by practically every source known to the author that treats Singapore in the early nineteenth century in some adequate sense.

15. J. Gallagher and R. Robinson, 'The Imperialism of Free Trade', *The Economic History Review*, Vol. VI, No. 1, August 1953.

16. Consider, as an example, the sources of revenue for the government of the Straits Settlements (Singapore was the capital and the most important of the three territories, the other two being Malacca and Penang), in the year from 1 May 1863 to 30 April 1864:

	£
Excise and other farms	137,521
Land and forests	6,705
Stamp tax	26,175
Law and justice	9,957
Public works	4,222
Marine	4,300
Miscellaneous	3,029
Total	191,909

Figures taken from Cameron, op. cit., p.209. Excise farms alone produced more than two-thirds of the revenue and were derived almost entirely from the Chinese population, the chief consumers of opium, spirits, etc. The Chinese would also be the chief contributors to the sum marked under law and justice, given that they had the most criminals.

17. It has been suggested by Jackson, op. cit., p.111, that the unfavourable land terms (which did not allow for long leases on land) before the 1830s discouraged European investment in commercial agriculture (the Chinese were not discouraged because theirs was an agriculture of quick returns, therefore short leases on the land were no matter. Moreover, they cultivated gambier and pepper independently of the British for some time). Other discouraging factors cited by Paul Wheatley in 'Land Use in the Vicinity of Singapore in the Eighteen-Thirties', *Malayan Journal of Tropical Geography*, Vol. 2, 1954, p.64, and G. W. Earl, *The Eastern Seas, or*

Voyages and Adventures in the Indian Archipelago, in 1832-33-34, comprising a tour of Java, visits to Borneo, the Malay peninsula, etc., also an account of the present state of Singapore (London, Allen and Co., 1837), p.64, were the inability of the police to protect planters in isolated settlements, the presence of tigers in the interior, and the lack of a suitable labour supply. Yet another possible reason was the warning by John Crawfurd, Resident of Singapore in 1825, that the soil of Singapore was sterile and almost useless. J. Crawfurd, 'Agriculture in Singapore', *Journal of Indian Archipelago*, iii (1849), reprinted from *Singapore Chronicle*, 1824. The real reason, however, was that little profit could be gained from commercial agriculture for the free traders as the British market had high tariffs. Later when the monopoly of the China trade by the East India Company was abolished and there was a prospect of lower tariffs for crops like gambier and sugar, the free traders moved in. They forced the government to bring about a suitable land system, developed the interior, and compelled the opening of Hongkong in 1842, thus allowing for mass migration to South-East Asia to create an ample labour supply (see Michael Greenberg, *British Trade and the Opening of China, 1800-42* (Cambridge University Press, 1951), and Wang Gungwu, *A Short History of the Nanyang Chinese* (Singapore, Eastern University Press Ltd., 1959), p.23.

18. This is not to say that the separate identity of the Chinese is exactly an objective way of viewing the problem, if a problem exists at all. There are other aspects, as far as much of the literature on the overseas Chinese in the 1950s and 60s is concerned, such as the economic strength of the overseas Chinese in comparison with that of the indigenous South-East Asians and their potential political strength. Thus, Morton Fried, writing of the Chinese in the Western hemisphere, noted that studies of the Chinese in South-East Asia were primarily concerned about their strategic commercial and potential political role, while those in the Western hemisphere were concerned with the extension of knowledge of the relations between culture and the formation of personality. 'Some Observations of the Chinese in British Guiana', by Morton Fried, in *Social and Economic Studies*, Vol. 5, No. 1, March 1956. But to those writing from the nationalistic point of view, a view which pervades the above-mentioned literature, the last two problems apparently cease to exist if the Chinese were to assimilate or were to lose their separate identity. The literature on their political role revolves mainly around Malaya and Singapore. See Lucian Pye: *Guerilla Communism in Malaya: Its Social and Political Meaning* (Princeton, Princeton University Press, 1956); Gene Z. Hanrahan, *The Communist Insurrection in Malaya: A Survey* (New York, Praeger, 1964); Anthony Short, 'Communism and the Emergency', in Wang Gungwu (ed.), *Malaysia* (New York, Praeger, 1964); K. J. Ratnam, *Communalism and the Political Process in Malaya* (Kuala Lumpur, University of Malaya, 1965). On the economic structure of the overseas Chinese, see N. Uchida, *The Overseas Chinese—A Bibliographical Essay based on the Resources of the Hoover Institution* (Palo Alto, Ca. Stanford University, Hoover Institution on War, Revolution and Peace, 1959); see also his 'Economic Activities of the Chinese in Southeast Asia', *Asian Affairs*, Vol. 1, No. 1, March 1956, edited and published by Asia Kiyokai, Japan.

19. G. W. Skinner, 'Change and Persistence in Chinese Culture Overseas: A Comparison of Thailand and Java', *Journal of South Seas Society*, xvi, (1960).

20. E. Wickberg, *The Chinese in Philippine Life* (New Haven, Yale University Press, 1966), p.241.

21. Barrington Moore, Jr., *Social Origins of Dictatorship and Democracy: Lord and Peasant in the Making of the Modern World* (Boston, Beacon Press, 1967). See his epilogue on 'Reactionary and Revolutionary Imagery'.

22. See W. E. Willmott, *The Political Structure of the Chinese Community in Cambodia* (London, University of London, Athlone Press, 1970), p.8.

23. See Chapter VI.

II

THE FREE TRADE SOCIETY AND THE GAMBIER AND PEPPER SOCIETY

THE British originally acquired Singapore in 1819 for two purposes. The first was to serve as an outpost for the protection of the British East India Company's trade with China and also for the protection of India. Singapore formed the last of three such outposts sought by the Company in the Malay Peninsula. Penang, founded in 1786, was the first, and second came Malacca, taken from the Dutch during the Napoleonic Wars but returned in 1818, and finally annexed with the Anglo-Dutch Treaty of 1824. The second purpose was to serve as a base for the conduct of free trade in South-East Asia. Two groups believed in this free trade: the country traders, people originally permitted by the Company to participate in some aspects of the Eastern trade, and the rising manufacturing interests in Britain. By the early nineteenth century, these country traders had made trading inroads into what the Dutch considered to be their economic preserve, the Indonesian islands. Meanwhile, the manufacturing interests, having destroyed the monopoly of the Company on the Indian trade, were increasingly ready also to challenge the Company's monopoly of the China trade. The Eastern archipelago, after all, was a potential market. Singapore was thus important to both groups.

But when the monopoly of the China trade of the Company was ended in the 1830s, a victory for these interests,[1] free trade became the dominant reason for the existence of Singapore. By then Singapore primarily served the purposes of the manufacturing interests, for it became essentially a sorting house for manufactured goods from Britain and produce from South-East Asia. Many of the country traders became the agents for these interests. Singapore's strategic location in South-East Asia, together with this policy of free trade, were to make it the dominant commercial centre of the area during the nineteenth century.

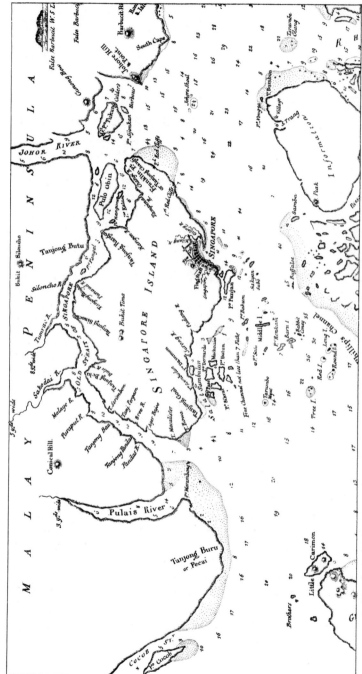

1. Singapore in the 1820s (From J. H. Moor, Notices of the Indian Archipelago and Adjacent Countries, Singapore, 1837)

Singapore was considered adequate, despite its small area, since the free traders needed only a base.[2] This was different from the 1870s when it was necessary for the industrial powers to seize as much territory as possible to form an outlet for investment.[3] The advantage of Singapore was that it commanded shipping from India to China passing through the Straits of Malacca, and at the same time it acted as a suitable centre from which the free traders could penetrate the market of the Malay archipelago.[4] To make this centre function, Chinese were allowed to migrate in great numbers because the British thought the indigenous people were not interested in commerce.[5] Before very long, the Chinese constituted the majority of the population, and consequently for our period Singapore can reasonably be termed a Chinese society.[6]

But the establishment of Singapore was not without profound social consequences. Singapore was not a *tabula rasa*. There was then already in existence another Chinese society, based on gambier and pepper agriculture, which free trade destroyed, though not without major social convulsions. Moreover, the newer Chinese society which developed from free trade was basically unstable. The fall-out from the gambier and pepper society combined with ever-increasing migration from China produced such a strain on this free trade society that it broke apart. Stability was not restored until the British intervention in the Malay Peninsula, which linked it politically with Singapore, and led both to heavier British regulation of this society on a considerable scale and an easing of the strains through renewed prosperity.

But before we argue out the linkage of free trade with the social convulsions, essentially by a careful examination of the four riots which were of the greatest intensity and magnitude before 1876, the stage has first to be set. Two chapters will be devoted to this task, and this one will be concerned with a description of the two Chinese societies, the free trade society and the gambier and pepper society, with the emphasis on the origins of their two dominant classes. The positions of these classes in the two economies and the kind of people they attracted will be considered. In the other, their social and political organizations will be analysed.

The Free Trade Society

First let us analyse the free trade economy in Singapore, and ask what was the mechanism which the manufacturing interests in Britain devised to get their industrial goods to this area?

This had two component parts. The first was meant to integrate an advanced economy with a backward one. The two main problems faced were how to reconcile a situation where the place of origin of capital, England, was separated by thousands of miles from the actual sphere of operations, and how to bridge the technical distance between the two economies. Today, such problems are to a great extent solved by the presence of capital-lending institutions in most parts of the globe which can make capital readily available where required, and by the existence of modernized urban sectors in the developing economies which supply the skills necessary to facilitate economic relations between the two. No such conditions obtained then, and the solution the interests devised was the system of agency houses. This involved the establishment of agents in places where the goods were to be sold. A network of such agents was established in India, Singapore, Batavia, and China. Where capital was lacking, goods were sold or exchanged in the developing economies for native produce, gold, specie, or for bills which could be discounted in one of the four places mentioned. Delivery of goods from Britain was by the consignment method whereby goods were dispatched to the agents to be stocked for ultimate disposal, not necessarily to order. (This was a function of the need to be rid of the surplus goods, and of the long time needed for an order made in South-East Asia to reach Britain.) The solution was very successful and thus the consignment system, according to Greenberg, formed 'the essential method of Manchester trade with the East and the agency house was its linchpin'.[7]

The second part involved the goods reaching the native consumers. That was not as easy as it sounds. While agents had a compelling interest in disposing rapidly of their goods (too many stocks involved expenses for maintenance, and, moreover, the more goods sold the more were the commissions), there were nevertheless limits to their push. They lacked the knowledge and the patience to deal with the indigenous population;[8] nor would the white man's prestige be enhanced if they were seen haggling with them. Some intermediary was necessary, and the Chinese were found to be suitable.[9]

On receiving a consignment, the agent would seek a Chinese to dispose of all or part of his consignment. Two kinds of arrangement were effected. One involved a barter-cum-credit system whereby there was either a straight exchange of goods with whatever the Chinese had, or the agent gave the Chinese credit, to be redeemed within a period of three to six months, depending on the mutual understanding, by some suitable Eastern produce such as coffee, sugar, pepper, tin, and so on. A promissory note was often extracted for surety. Such an arrangement, quite common in the early years of Singapore, was often honoured in the breach, according to European sources, mainly by the Chinese, and therefore the second arrangement, a straight payment of cash, was insisted on by many agents after 1835. However, the insistence was lessened whenever competition between the agents to dispose of their goods was keen.[10] After the arrangements were effected, the rest was up to the Chinese. Many were the ways in which the Chinese interacted economically with the natives. It will be sufficient to mention here three methods, the first being an aggressive pushing of business. A rather extreme account of this has been left on the record. A certain Paul Pry, after chiding his fellow Europeans for idleness while the Chinese merchants were busy cornering the market, wrote that:

. . . establishments have been formed in the Southern and Eastern extremities of the State of Johore/the state next to Singapore/coast, in which the Chinese have their respective agents, who are in almost daily communication with each other, who board all native vessels passing westward which they will not suffer to proceed until every article in them is bought, which is worth buying. When at length these prahus/boats/do anchor off our river, what do Europeans get from them? Nothing, gentlemen.[11]

A second method was less aggression and this involved the use of patience and adaptability to local Malay sensitivities such as were displayed by some businessmen, as a local Chinese writer, Tan Tek Soon, observed.[12] But the third method, probably the most common, was the market or the bazaar in Singapore, noted by contemporary writers[13] where Chinese, natives, *et al.*, descended to do business. In this interaction, the Chinese obtained the produce for which the goods were exchanged, either through barter or through the medium of money, and those basic necessities such as rice or salt, to sustain the population of the entrepôt.

From this, the structure for a Chinese mercantile class developed. Some precision in the definition of this class is here in order. We refer to the Chinese merchant class as the group of Chinese who were more or less directly involved in the export and import of commodities, that is, those Chinese who dealt directly with or who were employed by European agents who ultimately controlled the import and export sector. Observe that such a definition does not include what may be called the 'petty capitalists', the innumerable retailers and shopkeepers who occupied a less elevated position in the whole process of the entrepôt economy. Though they could be said to be involved in commercial activities, their position was not strategic and they were ultimately dependent on those Chinese who dealt directly with the European agents. Some were employed by the Chinese merchants and some did business independently but from all that is known of present overseas Chinese commercial society,[14] it is unlikely they made much money as petty businessmen.

Some estimate can be made of the number of Chinese merchants in our period. Obviously they increased as the years progressed but it is unlikely that they amounted to more than about a hundred at any time. One way to gauge this is by examining the number of European agents. The numbers of European firms (private European merchants all worked for firms) were as follows.[15]

1827	14
1846	22
1855	36
1858	44
1864	52
1867	60
1872	62

Working on the assumption that one firm did not do business with more than two Chinese merchants, since finding a trustworthy Chinese was most difficult and the volume of business was not so great as not to be capably handled by one or two intermediaries at the most, the number of such Chinese merchants probably did not exceed 124 by 1870. In view of the probability that some Chinese merchants worked for more than one agent,[16] the numbers should probably be far less. Certainly, the list given in the Colonial Directory of 1873[17] does not exceed 105. Who were the Chinese who became these merchants?

That can best be answered by first considering another question, what means did the European agents have to enforce agreements? This may seem an idle question today when the law and the police take care of that. In fact, however, the record is replete with many cases of abuse by the Chinese, such as absconding with goods and procuring inferior produce for the European agents instead of the expected quality.[18] Does the nature of the Singapore legal system account for this?

Though there was doubt about the legality of the various admin-
istrations in Singapore before 1827—before then the British Parliament had not ratified the annexation of Singapore and many Europeans did not consider themselves subject to whatever law might then
exist[19]—legally constituted courts came into existence soon after
1827. Law then became theoretically sovereign. Naturally the laws
passed governing business relations were based on the British
practice, given their political control of the island. But did the law
allow for loopholes? Were judicial interpretations of business
arrangements ambiguous? If both were so, it is not difficult to see
how shrewd Chinese, or for that matter, Europeans, could get round
both the spirit and the letter of the business agreements. On this
score, save for the bankruptcy law, introduced in the late 1840s by the
Indian Government and accepted reluctantly by the European mercantile community in Singapore, whereby a Chinese merchant could
send his assets back to China where they could not be impounded
if a bankruptcy was declared (such cases were few, however), the
law and its interpretation favoured the European. Many cases can
be cited;[20] the one appended is particularly instructive on the European judicial style.

In 1830, a certain Kong Tuan was successfully sued by a certain
Diggles on the grounds that a certain Ong Tuan, to whom Diggles
gave a considerable amount of goods and who absconded, was a
partner of Kong Tuan, though Kong Tuan denied it. Diggles'
case rested on the fact that 'in consequence of the high opinion
entertained of Kong Tuan by the European merchants, and *the
general impression that he was a partner of Ong Tuan*, the plaintiff
was induced to give the latter goods to a considerable amount,
which he never would have done, had he not believed Kong Tuan to
have been his partner.'[21] The magistrate accepted Diggles' argument on the grounds that there was no way in which European
merchants could judge the existence or otherwise of partnerships
among Chinese, since they were unacquainted with the Chinese
language. Subsequently, there was some European comment to
the effect that the decision was unfair. However, there was apparently nothing the Chinese could do about it, as seen by many
subsequent declarations in English in the *Singapore Chronicle* by
many Chinese merchants disavowing partnerships with certain
other Chinese. The point of this is that the law favoured European
cultural perceptions and that the Chinese knew they had to play
the game the European way.[22]

The law, then, was not in doubt. But its implementation was another matter. In the early years of Singapore there was essentially no way for the law governing business relations to be enforced if either partner was determined to break an arrangement. For one thing, the bureaucracy and the police were woefully inadequate even for their appointed tasks. The bureaucracy had their hands full extracting revenue from the Chinese population,[23] and, even if they had wanted to, they probably could not find the resources to ensure that business arrangements were honoured. The civil police, on the other hand, could not even keep the civil peace, let alone chase absconders. They could not, for example, do anything about crime in the interior of Singapore island, confined as they were to the city itself.

They were not aided by the free movement of Chinese between Singapore and the surrounding areas where the British writ did not yet extend, and, of course, China. Had the Chinese been strictly confined to Singapore, they would have been less tempted to abscond. No such fear of future punishment awaited a Chinese who absconded; he could simply disappear into any of these Chinese communities; for the only recourse the British had was to appeal to the local political authorities. There was no guarantee of a proper response. Such cases were many. The records show, for example, a rather plaintive letter by certain British merchants in Penang urging the British authorities to petition the rulers of Kedah and Trang, Siam and Pahang, to do something about Chinese seeking a haven in their states.[24] One might also add that these merchants, for good measure, also urged the British authorities in Malacca and Singapore to be more vigilant themselves.

But somehow, despite the lack of enforcement, and the abuse, the system worked—as the trade figures indicate. This must be explained. Early in the game, many astute Europeans saw that the basic ingredient for making the system work was not the law or its implementation, but mutual trust and confidence between business partners. When Singapore was newly established in 1820, the famous scholar and later administrator of Singapore, Crawfurd, states that inexperienced traders of European origin should best dispose of their goods to the indigenous population through 'an intermediate class in which both can repose confidence'.[25] Even ten years later, that ingredient was still vital, as seen by the words of the British magistrate in the Diggles case. He gave as another reason for the conviction of Kong Tuan that

. . . if the plea of the defendant [Kong Tuan] be admitted, it would open the door to extensive fraud and swindling, and place property on a precarious footing, and put an end to the confidence between European and native [Chinese] merchants, the liberal exercise of which has so much accelerated the mercantile prosperity of this settlement.[26]

Such a viewpoint was to develop into a refrain in the writings of many Europeans.

Obviously the European agents did not ascertain the trustworthiness of a Chinese middleman by feelings alone. There must be a more sure, objective basis. In the context of a pioneer Chinese society in Singapore, so culturally different from the West and possessing so many adventurers, those Chinese with some westernization and some roots in the area would make more appealing partners than those Chinese with none. For, as the Diggles case demonstrated, a major cause of misunderstanding arose from the different cultural backgrounds of both sides. That could be reduced if the Chinese had some understanding of Western ways. In this connexion, one of the more knowledgeable British writers in the nineteenth century told his fellow Europeans of the advisability of doing business with a group of Chinese called the Malacca Chinese. 'They,' he wrote, 'are more enlightened and make better merchants. Many of this class who have been educated at the Malacca College, speak English tolerably well, and, from their constant communication with the Europeans they have acquired in some measure their habits and modes of transacting business, which renders them more agreeable to the latter than those who have not enjoyed similar advantages.'[27]

Moreover, if a Chinese middleman had something tangible, like real property or family in Singapore and the surrounding areas, especially those under British control, he would think twice before running away with the goods. This was recognized by the European mercantile community. From their paper, the *Singapore Chronicle*, let us consider this, which, unedifying as the account of the Chinese may be, nevertheless deserves quotation at some length because it describes well the spirit of the times:

From the nature of the trade of this place and the manner in which business is conducted, the great inconvenience and risk of property attendant upon this state of things must be evident, as the majority of the Chinese, and other native merchants to whom the Europeans are obliged to dispose of their property, and generally at long credits, are men of little or no capital, and as they can at any time obtain credit to a much greater amount than that of their outstanding debts, they have every inducement to act dishonestly, particularly is the case at present, when they can do so with impunity, by openly leaving the place and setting their creditors at defiance. From our knowledge of the native buyers, however, we do not think there are many here who would be guilty of such an act of barefaced robbery, although we have little doubt but there are amongst them who would not scruple to have recourse to any measure by which they thought they could make money. Not many weeks ago, we are informed, some of our Chinese merchants (natives of China) converted everything they had in their possession into dollars, and returned to China with the proceeds by the junks in the most open manner, without paying a single debt. *The principal part of the resident Chinese here, however, are natives of Malacca, and are generally possessed of some little property there, although there is not so much fear of their decamping in this manner* [author's italics], they take advantage of our present situation, and trade with the funds they ought to apply in the liquidation of their just debts, knowing that they cannot legally be compelled to part with a single dollar.[28]

Consequently, the European agents, in order to reduce their risks, would settle on Chinese possessing the assets mentioned above and such Chinese were strategically placed to enter the ranks of the upper middlemen or merchants. Were such Chinese spread evenly over the Chinese population or were they drawn from any special group among the Chinese? Contemporary writers observed that the richest Chinese and those who had a disproportionate number of merchants in their ranks were from a group called the Malacca Chinese,[29] whose existence has been referred to in the two preceding quotations. (This was the name given to the Chinese immigrants from Chinese communities that had been domiciled in the Malay Peninsula for some time, since the overwhelming number of these had come from Malacca.)

The writers' observations were accurate, for the Malacca Chinese were outstanding compared to other Chinese in their possession of the assets needed for business success in Singapore. Descended originally from Chinese who came from southern Fukien and forming a continuous colony in Malacca from even before the Portuguese conquest in 1511, the Malacca Chinese, according to a local Chinese scholar, Lim Boon Keng,[30] were exposed to a great degree of westernization from the successive conquests of Malacca by the Portuguese, Dutch, and British. Many developed some knowledge of one of the European languages, particularly English, and also developed friendships with many Englishmen, which stood them in good stead in Singapore, since some of these Englishmen became important officials there in the early years. For example, Farquhar, the first Resident of Singapore, had previously been the Resident of Malacca, and he left records saying that many from Malacca followed him when he left for Singapore.[31] Raffles himself spent some time in Malacca before Singapore, and it is likely that he developed friendships with some Chinese there. Needless to say, long years of domicile in Malacca made some Chinese grow roots there; what property, family, and sentiments they had, were probably also located there.[32]

Immigrants direct from China possessed no such assets and thus the Malacca Chinese won hands down. There was yet another asset which the latter had, a knowledge of the language and customs of the Malays in the area. Many of the Malacca Chinese spoke Malay, some indeed better than Chinese. They were thus at a great advantage when it came to doing business with the Malays.

For some evidence more rigorous than the above observations, however, the names of the Chinese merchants listed in the *Straits Directory*,[33] a publication of the European mercantile community in Singapore, have been examined. The years checked are from 1846 (the earliest year for which there are records in the Singapore National Library) to 1873, just before the British intervention in the Malay Peninsula. Detailed information could not be found for all the merchants despite a diligent search. But the bulk of those for whom such information is available were either from Malacca or were connected with the Malacca Chinese through marriage, friendship, or business partnerships. Below are the merchants for which information could be found (1846 to 1872):

Tan Kim Seng	Malacca-born
Hoo Ah Kay, alias Whampoa	China-born but had relatives in Penang, a British-controlled state in the Malay Peninsula
See Eng Wat	Malacca-born
Lim Seng Chai	had a son, Lim Soon Yang, who married a granddaughter of Tan Kim Seng from Malacca
Chee Teang Why	had a plantation in Malacca, indicating Malacca ties, and was probably born in Malacca
See Eng Wai	Malacca-born
See Eng Guan	ditto
See Tek Guan	ditto

Low Thuan Loke	Singapore-born[34]
Tang Eng Siew	known to have a business partnership with a Malacca Chinese
Tan Tock Seng	Malacca-born
Tan Kim Cheng	son of Tan Tock Seng
Seah Eu Chin	China-born, but early developed a friendship with a Malacca Chinese called Kim Swee
Tan Beng Swee	son of Tan Kim Seng
Hooding Brothers	all Malacca-born
Tan Kim Tian	Straits-born
Lee Cheng Tee	Malacca-born

In 1873, the *Colonial Directory* (a European-published directory) gave an unusually long list of Chinese merchants. There were altogether 105 names listed as the 'principal Chinese traders dealing with Europeans'. Information could only be found for twenty-seven of them but all presented a similar picture. They are as follows:

Ang Kim Cheak	son of Malacca-born Chinese, Ang Choon Seng
Chia Lek	China-born, but had a business partnership with a Malacca Chinese called Kho Tek See
Chong Ann Beeh	Malacca-born
Cheang Hong Lim	Singapore-born
Tan Hock Eng	Straits-born
Koh Eng Hoon	Malacca-born
Lim Leack	China-born, but had a Straits-born wife
Tan Chin Seng	Malacca-born
Lee Cheng Yan	ditto
Lim Keng Guan	ditto
Lim Lan	had a business partnership with a Malacca Chinese, Cheong Ann Bee
Ong Chong Chiew	Singapore-born
Ong Ewe Hai	Malacca-born
Tan Kwee Lan	Straits-born
Teo Kit	China-born but had a business partnership with Cheang Hong Lim
Wee Bin	China-born
Wee Ah Hood	Malacca-born
Seah Eu Chin	See previous list
Tan Seng Poh	brother-in-law of Seah Eu Chin and originating from Perak in the Malay Peninsula
Seah Choo Seah	son of Seah Eu Chin
Low Ah Jit	China-born

Chua Moh Choon	no relevant information except known to be a secret society leader
Tan Yong Siak	China-born
Boey Ah Ghee	China-born, but known to have made friends with a European called J. Guthrie
Yow Lup Nam	China-born, but old friend of Whampoa
Wong Ah Siak	China-born

As a check against these lists the *Singapore Free Press* and the *Straits Times* were scanned for data about any Chinese merchants. It was found that the names of Chinese merchants kept appearing in addresses to important government officials on state and social occasions. Here, two such addresses are examined from two different periods. One was made to a departing Mr. A.L. Johnston, a famous merchant in 1841. Information could be found for five of the Chinese merchants who signed.[35] They were:

Chee Teang Why	see previous list
Yeoh Kim Swee	Malacca-born
Seah Eu Chin	see previous list
Chan Koo Chan	China-born, but married to a daughter of Tan Tock Seng from Malacca
Lim Lan	see previous list

In 1877, thirty-two Chinese merchants' names appeared before a list of names that followed the name of the Gambier and Pepper Society over an address welcoming the new governor.[36] Information could be found for fourteen of these. They were:

Hoo Ah Kay, alias Whampoa	see previous list
Tan Kim Cheng	ditto
Seah Eu Chin	ditto
Tan Seng Poh	ditto
Tan Beng Swee	ditto
Tan Yeok Nee	China-born, but had business partnerships with Tan Seng Poh and Cheang Hong Lim
Seah Choo Seah	see previous list
Khoo Cheng Teong	China-born
Tan Soon Toh	son of Tan Kim Cheng
Ong Kew Ho	see previous list
Goh Siew Siew	China-born
Lim Tiang Swee	worked for a Malacca Chinese, Lim King Wan

| Khoo Tiong Poh | had a business partnership with Malacca Chinese, Cheong Ann Bee |
| Lee Cheng Gum | Malacca-born |

Should the reader sense a certain circularity in the above argument, two sources in Chinese will corroborate. The first is the Hokkien Temple called the Thian Hok Keng which was essentially the earliest organizational expression of the solidarity of the Hokkien dialect group. This group was without doubt the richest of all the dialect groups in Singapore. The temple, for example, cost 30,000 Spanish dollars when built in 1840.[37] This figure is comparable to the total amount of money per year sent by all the Chinese in Singapore to China which, according to one writer, ranged from 30,000 Spanish dollars in some years to about 70,000 Spanish dollars in others.[38] This amount is all the more impressive when one recalls that remittances to China amounted to an almost religious duty for most Chinese,[39] while contributing to a temple was rather lukewarmly done. Hence those few merchants who raised money to build the temple must have been very rich men. A plaque in the Temple dated around 1865 lists eleven members of the committee of management of the Temple. Data could be obtained for only six of these. But five of them were Malacca Chinese or were known to be connected with them, and it is likely that the sixth was similarly connected. They were:[40]

Tan Beng Swee	son of Tan Kim Seng from Malacca
See Moh Guan	from Malacca
Koh Eng Hoon	from Malacca
Khoo Cheng Tiong	origins unknown, probably from Malacca. However, one of his sons married a descendant of a Malacca Chinese, Si Hood Kay
Tan Kim Tian	descended from Malacca Chinese
Tan Quee Lan	origins unknown, but his name was in a petition protesting against a certain measure of the government, the majority of the petitioners being Malacca Chinese

The second source relates to one of the richest and most powerful clans in Singapore, the Tans. The *Nan-yang nien-chien*[41] listed two founders, Tan Kim Cheng and Tan Beng Swee, and both were Malacca Chinese.

There was another important source of capital accumulation— the rights to monopolies on opium, gambling, drinking, and so on.

The most lucrative of these was opium. According to a Dr. Little who apparently did intense research into the opium situation in the 1840s, those who made big money were those who obtained such rights from the government.[42] They were called the opium farmers who amounted to more than one in a single year.[43] Opium rights were obtained in two ways, by private agreement and by competitive bidding.[44] It is very likely that both worked to the advantage of the Malacca Chinese. Thus in a private agreement, all things being equal, the Malacca Chinese would be more favoured than other Chinese. As to the latter, the rents would be so high as to prevent any but the richest from succeeding in the bidding and in possessing the capital to buy the opium. Consider the monthly rent for the opium rights from the years 1822 to 1867.[45]

TABLE I

MONTHLY RENT FOR OPIUM RIGHTS, 1822-1867

Year	Monthly Rent ($)	Year	Monthly Rent ($)
1822-3	1,615	1835-6	4,800
1823-4	2,960	1836-7	4,570
1824-5	1,925	1837-8	4,570
1825-6	2,032	1838-9	4,860
1826-7	2,050	1839-40	4,050
1827-8	2,060	1840-1	5,440
1828-9	2,720	1841-2	6,250
1829-30	2,060	1842-3	6,347
1830-1	3,270	1843-4	8,990.45
1831-2	2,960	1844-5	8,990.45
1832-3	3,440	1845-6	8,990.45
1832-3	3,440	1845-6	8,991.35
1833-4	4,000	1846-7	7,500
1834-5	5,000		

Consider, by contrast, the wages of the average labourer per month which in those rare good years might be as high as $15, though they went as low as $3.[46] Obviously no labourer could dream of buying the rights let alone gaining the capital to buy the opium wholesale.

Those in a position to make money from the various farms had to be already themselves very rich. At this time, the rich could only be the merchants. Scanning the *Straits Directory*, the *Singapore Chronicle*, and the *Journal of the Indian Archipelago*, three farmers were found for whom there is information. They were Choa Chong

Long and Kong Tuan, opium farmers, and Tan Che San, a gambling farmer. We know that they were all merchants and were Malacca Chinese or assimilated into them.

In addition to the new Chinese merchant class, the entrepôt economy sustained three other classes in the new Chinese society. (Here class is defined as those who occupy a definite position in the relations of production.) One consisted of those, here termed petty merchants for convenience, who were involved in petty commercial activities and who were not directly involved in the export and import sector. These petty merchants were divided into two groups; those who were involved in the continuation of the process whereby surplus goods were exchanged for produce with the indigenous population, and those who were the retailers primarily for the Chinese population in Singapore, particularly for those involved in commercial agriculture, to whom they supplied rice, clothing, and other necessities, and collected from them agricultural produce, mainly gambier and pepper.

A second class consisted of those who were involved in crafts. These were the carpenters, builders of boats, ships, and houses, and so on. From what could be gathered, they pursued these crafts as professions and not part-time while farming or doing something else. Their existence was precarious for they were dependent on the expanding entrepôt economy and not on any stable institution.

Lastly, there was a third class composed of those who were neither artisans nor involved in commercial activities, but contributed their unskilled labour to the entrepôt economy, for example, as porters at the docks, casual labourers, domestic servants, or street vendors. Their existence was the most precarious of all for it was subject not only to the fluctuations of the entrepôt economy but also to an increasing migrant population as unskilled as they were.

Our classification may be compared with others made by contemporary observers. Three of these exist, made at different dates. A government survey of 1827 shows that out of a Chinese population of 5,743 males, 1,222 were agriculturists, 2,742 were involved in commerce, 1,349 were artisans, 427 were servants and coolies, and 3 were boatmen and fishermen.[47]

Twenty-two years later the government census of 1849 reveals a population of 24,790 Chinese, of whom 98 were merchants and clerks, 2,322 mechanics, 8,426 agriculturists, 8,303 labourers, 335 servants and other miscellaneous.[48] However, to this the *Singapore*

Free Press made a slight correction, stating that some of the population should be labelled as commercial people, such as shopkeepers and traders,[49] a group which presumably the census placed in either the categories of mechanics or labourers. Finally, one observer, on the basis of visits made to Singapore from 1854 to 1862, wrote that among the Chinese population were the wealthiest merchants, the agriculturists in the interior, the mechanics, and labourers.[50]

If agriculture is left out, our classification basically accords with these three, the only point at issue being that those who were involved in small-scale commercial activities, the petty merchants, were included in the 1827 census with the Chinese merchants, and probably included with either the mechanics or the labourers in the 1849 census, and also in the findings of the private observer. This is not difficult to explain. Some who might appear to be commercial people to one census taker, because they were involved in retail activities, might appear as labourers or workers to another, because many of these petty retailers would probably have performed manual tasks while retailing or trading when carrying goods to their own stores. Such performers of manual work could easily be considered as labourers by Europeans, few of whom were known for any particular precision in distinguishing components of the Chinese population. It may be assumed that 'mechanics' refers to our artisan class, since motor-vehicles or tankers for mechanics to repair did not then exist.[51]

The Gambier and Pepper Society

Of that other older Chinese society in Singapore we have some evidence from scattered English sources. In 1822, a traveller to Singapore wrote to the newspaper, the *Singapore Chronicle*, that he was 'astonished to find so large a population of Chinese, Bugis, Malays and others comfortably settled and industriously employed on the island'.[52] This could not have been the population which developed from British free trade, for Singapore, in British terms, had hardly been in existence for three years. Given the slow means of Chinese and native communication then, it would take many more years for a population to settle in response to British policy. Hence this population must have existed before 1819. It is reasonably certain from the account of another English observer that an independent Chinese settlement existed. Earl wrote from 1832-4 that this settlement was 'a few miles distant from the town, which is said to be very populous, and as considerable quantities of produce are brought thence to the town for sale, their plantations must be very extensive'.[53] The size of their population was estimated in 1835 by the *Singapore Chronicle* to be about 3,000.[54]

Apparently it was a settlement of some significance for, according to a recent researcher, this settlement had begun by 1827 to replace Rhio as the commercial centre of gambier in the Malay archipelago,[55] while from a Chinese perspective the settlement also acted as a kind of centre, if not a base, for the Chinese, who plied their junks mainly along the coastal areas of Indo-China, Siam, the Malay Peninsula, and Borneo, in the South China Sea and then to other parts of the Malay archipelago.[56] Thus both Purcell and P'an Hsing-nung may have been correct when the former suggested that the Chinese in this settlement came from Rhio while the latter stated that many Chinese had also come from Siam.[57]

The mainstays of the old Chinese economy were gambier and pepper. They must have been cultivated extensively, for a letter to the editor of the *Asiatic Journal* in 1821 mentioned that the 'spice gardens in Singapore already bid fair to rival those of the neighbouring islands'.[58] By 1832-6, as mentioned above, Earl wrote of extensive plantations being found. The gambier produced before the 1830s was primarily exported to China.[59]

How did this gambier and pepper economy function? It followed the plantation system. The plantations, however, were not large scale, each generally employed only about 9 or 10 men, while a plantation of more than 12 or 13 men was considered a full complement. No plantation had more than 20 employees.[60] Three groups of people were involved, the financier, the pioneer planter, and the workers who were paid wages by the pioneer.

The pioneer who wished to start a plantation first approached a Chinese financier (usually a shopkeeper) for a stake. The terms of the arrangement might vary but essentially they would consist of the pioneer pledging his plantation and a proportion of his crop to the financier, with conditions favouring the latter, until the debt was discharged. Sometimes the financier insisted that the pioneer sold his entire crop to him. It is known in Penang that the financier insisted on a half-share in the plantation after it had existed for three years,[61] and that in Johore the pioneer had to obtain his provisions through the financier.[62] On the assumption that what basically obtained in Penang and Johore obtained also in Singapore and that under a pioneer economy with all its attendant risks a financier would tighten the screws whenever possible, we can assume that Singapore financiers did likewise.

There were then two other tasks to be performed, the search for land and workers. The first presented no legal difficulties for, before the 1830s, the British did not interfere at all beyond a two-mile radius from the town, despite claiming sovereignty over the whole island.[63] The evidence is not clear whether any Malay ruler would have exercised effective sovereignty on that part of the island with which the British did not interfere.[64] Even if they did, it is likely, judging from the experience of Johore in the latter half of the nineteenth century, that the Chinese would be given considerable leeway in the search for pioneer land. However, the Chinese had to consider ease of transportation to the town in such a search, since the crops were to be exported. Hence, it is likely that many in the beginning chose spots near the rivers or the coast, since water transport was considered easier than trekking through jungle. But in time many plantations were to be located near footpaths, for in 1827 the Resident Councillor, John Prince, observed gambier being brought 'to market on men's shoulders', presumably on foot.[65]

Labour could be found among those Chinese who came from Rhio, but in the main it was drawn from those who came from China by junk. Some came as free immigrants, paying their own passages, while others came by the credit ticket system. Under this system, the owner of a junk paid the travel expenses of an immigrant who was then bonded to him. On arrival the immigrant was kept under his control until someone came to 'buy' him off for a satisfactory sum, usually more than the expenses incurred so as to leave a margin of profit to the junk owner. The terms with the new 'buyer' usually consisted of working for a year for a subsistence allowance and no wages. The pioneer could be one of the 'buyers', and when the indebted immigrant became free, he could restart the process by becoming a pioneer.

Which among these three groups made the money? Not the workers, for they ultimately obtained the rawest deal. Their wages were fixed according to the prices of the two crops, and good wages could thus be cancelled by bad ones. Not only was insecurity their lot, they also lived very harsh and unpleasant lives. Housing was poor, and innumerable diseases such as beri-beri and malaria plagued them.

Any money left after basic necessities were taken care of could not have been much. Many sent remittances back to their families in China, and many also frittered it away on opium, which was run independently—and clandestinely—of the British.[65] It was often addictive, for in 1848 one writer noted that many workers 'brave death [from tigers] only that they may obtain the means of indulging themselves in the luxury of opium smoking'.[67]

It is also unlikely that the majority of the pioneers made much money. It was difficult enough to make the plantation operate let alone make a profit. Even if profitable, the pioneer had still to repay his loan with an interest that could be crushing. The *Singapore Free Press* in 1839 judged that about two-thirds of the plantations probably did not succeed, while most of the remaining one-third barely paid their way.[68]

Consequently, those who made the killing were the financiers. First, they made money from the export of the gambier: given the fact that it went to China by Chinese junks, they would have had some kind of working relationship with the owners of the junks.[69] Second, they would derive a high rate of interest from their advances to the pioneers, for the advances were often in clothes and provisions sold at higher than market price and at high interest. Where the debts were unpaid, the financiers would appropriate their plantations.[70] Moreover, many of these financiers were shopkeepers, and if the experience of the plantations in Johore is anything to go by, it is very likely that essential supplies such as rice went to the workers via the financiers.[71] These financiers, because of their probable links with the owners of the junk, would have a share in whatever money could be made in the traffic of coolies and the remittance of money back to China.[72]

Finally it needs only to be said that some of these financiers probably originated from Rhio, some were the very few pioneers who had become very successful and as a consequence could become financiers themselves.[73] They were primarily members of the Teochew dialect group.[74]

1. Those who pushed the hardest for free trade and eventually won were the cotton and wool interests. The introduction of large-scale machinery to their industry had brought about a surplus; the expense involved necessitated a constant increase in output, for profits came about only by lowering the cost per unit of production. Outlets had to be sought for this surplus. Hence restrictions had to go. See Greenberg, *British Trade*, p.146.

2. See 'Imperialism of Free Trade', by J. Gallagher and R. Robinson in *The Economic History Review*, Vol. VI, No. I, August 1953 for such an argument. The

author sees free trade as no less imperialistic when there was a large-scale grabbing of colonies by the European powers from the 1870s onwards.

3. See C.A. Bodelsen, *Studies in Mid-Victorian Imperialism* (London, Heinemann, 1960), pp.79-87, on the British fear of rivalry by the industrial powers on the continent, fully developed by the late nineteenth century. This fear led Britain to abandon free trade and to annex colonies.

4. Though Singapore was founded as early as 1819, it was not until the 1840s that free trade began to make an impact. See the map on p.12, probably drawn in 1825 but reproduced in 1837, the suggestion being that the publishers in 1837 thought 1825 features still obtained.

In this map, the trading station would seem not too significant, confined as it was to an extremely small corner of the island. That the map does not show an independent gambier and pepper settlement in the interior reveals the general ignorance of this settlement on the part of the Europeans. The map is taken from J. H. Moor, *Notices of Indian Archipelago and Adjacent Countries* (Singapore, 1837).

5. See a letter in the *Singapore Chronicle*, 15 February 1827, which states that in Singapore it is possible 'to assimilate the Asiatic (meaning Chinese) and the European very closely in the pursuits of commerce . . . here you stumble at every step over the produce of China . . .'.

6. The people who came to form the bulk of the population in Singapore were Chinese. Chinese had historically migrated to South-East Asia for trade and to small colonies to produce crops for the market in China. But it was with the Western colonization of South-East Asia that large-scale migration took place. As far as the British were concerned, that began with their policy of free trade which was to attract ever-increasing numbers of Chinese to Singapore. They came to serve as middlemen between the British and the natives of South-East Asia and to provide the labour in many of the plantations and mines which were opening up. By the latter half of the nineteenth century they formed more than half the population of Singapore.

7. Greenberg, op. cit., p.145.

8. See Earl, *The Eastern Seas*, p.186, for some comments about the need for Europeans to be patient when dealing with the indigenous population.

9. Ibid., p.416. He said that the British rarely had commercial intercourse with the natives. It is done 'by Chinese who have better acquaintance and patience into all the details of bargaining and weighing the goods'. See also *Singapore Chronicle*, 15 February 1827.

10. This paragraph is based on information from Wong Lin Ken, 'The Trade of Singapore, 1819-1869', *Journal of Royal Asiatic Society (Malayan Branch)*, Vol. 33, Part 4, No. 192, 1960; and an unpublished honours academic exercise, 'Singapore Agency Houses 1819-1900', by Loh Wen Fong, University of Malaya (Singapore), 1958, and relevant issues of the *Singapore Chronicle*.

11. *Singapore Chronicle*, 1 July 1830.

12. 'Chinese Local Trade', Tan Tek Soon, *Straits Chinese Magazine*, Vol. VI, March 1902, No. 23, p.91.

13. See *Singapore Chronicle*, 13 August 1829.

14. See T'ien Ju-Kang, *The Chinese in Sarawak, A Study of Social Structure* (Department of Anthropology, London School of Economics and Political Science, 1951).

15. Taken from Wong, 'Trade of Singapore', p.167.

16. Ibid., p.164.

17. Published by the *Straits Times*.

18. Examples are found in these issues of the *Singapore Chronicle*, 13 August 1829; 12 August 1830; 21 February 1835; 27 June 1835. See also letter from Bonham to Murchison in the *Straits Settlements Secret Correspondence* in the India Office

(London, 11 October 1825).

19. Crawfurd, the Resident, in his dispatch to the Supreme Government on 1 July 1823, wrote that the Europeans were 'at present amenable to no authority at this place and the ill-disposed had it always in their power to set the authority of government at defiance, and to render themselves a bane to the peaceful inhabitants. There exists no means whatever in civil cases of affording the natives any redress against them, nor in criminal cases of any remedy short of sending them for trial before the Supreme Court of Calcutta.' Dispatch found in Buckley, *An Anecdotal History*, p.164.

20. See *Singapore Chronicle*, 22 May 1828 and 12 August 1830.

21. Taken from *Singapore Chronicle*, 12 August 1830. Author's italics.

22. It would seem that around this period the Chinese did business on a personal basis. By that is meant that in their dealings with both Europeans and other Chinese, they did not establish companies on the European model, companies which had their own capital for surety and not the personal assets of the partners and shareholders in the company. Partnerships under the Chinese system were probably drawn from the family and close friends. Thus in Song, *One Hundred Years*, pp.46, 51, and 91, the earliest years where mention is made of the existence of Chinese limited companies (Kim Seng and Co., Chong San Seng Chai and Co., and Whampoa and Co.) were around 1840 and earlier. But they could not be earlier than 1827, for in a list of fifty Chinese subscribers to the Raffles monument (*Singapore Chronicle*, 15 March 1827), not one was a limited company, though four were listed as *kongsis*. (In this list, any firm or person who was anybody would have contributed.)

Now misunderstanding could easily arise in business done in this way, as partnerships were not explicitly spelled out in the Western sense and there was no legal mechanism to compel a presumed partner to pay for another who might have defaulted. But, judging from the fact that this had worked for about twenty years in Singapore and even longer in China, the customary sanctions against friends and family members practising bad faith must have been effective. However, when this system clashed with the Western system, the opportunities for bad faith and misunderstanding became very great. For example, a Chinese, possessing a partner under the Chinese system, could disavow any liability for him on the grounds that they were not partners in the Western sense. Or, to take what might appear to be a contrived example, a European, used though he might be to the Western system, could give a loan to a Chinese under the impression that this Chinese had a rich partner under the Chinese system and this European could then hold that rich partner liable for the loan, even though, strictly speaking, the two Chinese were not partners. That, of course, is what Diggles did.

The final authorities were the British and they were not necessarily fair, particularly so here with the magistrate. Because he was not convicting on the basis of the Western legal system nor even necessarily on the Chinese system (he could not possibly do that because, as he admitted, he knew no Chinese nor was he conversant with Chinese customs) but simply on the basis of the European's impression. The Chinese, of course had to give in as seen by the spate of declarations in a European newspaper, the *Singapore Chronicle*.

But it must not be assumed the Chinese went all the way. For the solution adopted (which, by the way, still applied even up to today) was, with regard to dealings with the Europeans or the state, to adopt the Western system, but among themselves, the Chinese system. In other words, Europeans could only hold the limited companies of the Chinese liable and not Chinese personally. Chinese, however, could hold each other personally liable. How the Chinese could maintain such a sub-system in face of the fact that unscrupulous Chinese could default and seek refuge in the Western system must be due to dialect and clan ties, the difficulty of defaulting and so on.

There still remains the question. Why maintain such a hybrid system? The answer is that as far as the Chinese were concerned, that system had always worked among themselves: so why change it, with all the problems associated with adaptation? They conceded only when they had no choice, i.e., in dealing with the European. This may sound conservative but the author thinks it is far from that. In a pioneer economy such as early Singapore and later in the Malay Peninsula, the risks associated with lending money were obviously very great. Money-lenders would be less inclined to lend to limited companies which could always fold up if they were not doing well. Whereas if the lenders knew the partners were personally liable and therefore would be careful with the management of the loan, these lenders might be more willing to give credit.

The *kongsis* in the 1827 list probably referred to the Teochews in the gambier and pepper agriculture, the Teochew financiers making the contributions in the name of the *kongsis*. (See Chapter VI.)

23. A cursory reading of the early government records will show that in so far as the bureaucracy was concerned about anything, it was with the extraction of revenue.

24. *Straits Settlements Records*, 13 May 1824.

25. J. Crawfurd, *History of the Indian Archipelago Containing an Account of the Manners, Arts, Languages, Religions, Institutions and Commerce of Its Inhabitants* (Edinburgh, A. Constable and Co.), p.263.

26. *Singapore Chronicle*, 12 August 1830.

27. Earl, *The Eastern Seas*, p.363.

28. *Singapore Chronicle*, 13 August 1829.

29. See Seah Eu Chin, 'The Chinese in Singapore', *Journal of the Indian Archipelago*, II, 1848, p.290, and the 'Notes on the Chinese in the Straits', *Journal of the Indian Archipelago*, Vol. IX, 1855. The author, J. Bradley, said that the Malacca Chinese had 'a virtual monopoly (of economic opportunities) in Singapore', p.115.

30. A. Wright and H. A. Cartwright (eds.), *Twentieth Century Impressions of Hong Kong, Shanghai, and Other Treaty Ports of China, their History, People, Commerce, Industries, and Resources* (London, Lloyd's Greater Britain Pub. Co., 1908), pp.876-7.

31. *Asiatic Journal and Monthly Register* (London, Allen and Co., May 1830), p.142.

32. It was common practice among the Malacca Chinese to retire to Malacca after a career in Singapore. The immigrants from China sought to retire to China instead. See the *Malacca Weekly Chronicle*, 3 November 1888, for one such example, a Malacca Chinese by the name of See Boon Tiang.

33. A publication of the *Straits Times*. The *Straits Directory* was probably the only one of its kind in the nineteenth century. See footnote 43 with regard to information about the occupations of the merchants.

34. Those born in Singapore would be similar to the Malacca Chinese with regard to the possession of the assets mentioned. Sometimes, a merchant is listed as Straits-born which means he was born in the Straits Settlements.

35. See *Singapore Free Press*, 23 December 1841.

36. *Singapore Free Press*, 27 October 1877.

37. See Comber, *Chinese Temples in Singapore* (Singapore, Eastern University Press, 1958), p.59.

38. 'Annual Remittances by Chinese Immigrants in Singapore to their Families in China', *Journal of the Indian Archipelago*, Vol. 1, 1847, p.35.

39. Ibid., p.35.

40. Copied from the Thian Hok Keng Temple in Teluk Ayer Street, Singapore. It is also found in Ch'en Yu-sung (Tan Yoek Seong) and Ch'en Ching Ho, *Hsin-chia-po hua-wen pei-ming chi-lu* (*Collection of Chinese Inscriptions in Singapore*), Hongkong,

1973. Information on merchants taken from Song, *One Hundred Years*.

41. *Nan-yang nien-chien (Nanyang yearbook)*, Singapore, 1951.

42. 'Modes of Using Opium', R. Little, *Journal of the Indian Archipelago*, Vol. 11, 1848.

43. See 'Provisions of the Opium Regulations for Singapore and Hongkong', *Journal of the Indian Archipelago*, Vol. II, 1848.

44. Ibid.

45. 'Modes of Using Opium', op. cit., p.50.

46. 'The Chinese Protectorate in Singapore, Events and Conditions Leading to its Establishment 1823-77', No. 16, 1960 of the *Journal of South Seas Society*, p.61.

47. *Straits Settlements Record*: 'Singapore Diary', 1 June 1827.

48. 'Census of Singapore made in months of November and December, 1849', *Journal of the Indian Archipelago*, Vol. IV, 1850, page facing 106.

49. *Singapore Free Press*, 5 March 1850.

50. Alfred R. Wallace, *The Malay Archipelago: The Land of the Orang Utan, and the Bird of Paradise* (New York, Harper and Brothers, 1869), p.32.

51. The government did not know much about the Chinese before 1877, for before then they did not have many officials who knew the Chinese language. See L. A. Mills, *British Malaya 1826-67*, reprinted (Kuala Lumpur, Oxford University Press, 1966), p.212. Unfortunately, the Hobson-Jobson Glossary of Anglo-Indian words and phrases by H. Yule and A. C. Burnell (New Delhi, 1903) does not contain the word 'mechanic'.

52. *The Penang Register and Miscellany*, 16 January 1822. See also a letter by Farquhar dated 23 December 1822 in 'Population of Singapore in 1819' by W. Bartley, *Journal of Royal Asiatic Society (Malayan Branch)*, December 1933, Vol. XI, Part II, p.177 that the 'first hill lying to the northward of the Government Hill is that of Selligie which in clearing the country at the commencement of the establishment was found to be occupied on the Western side by a Chinese planter who had formed a gambier plantation there'.

53. Earl, op. cit., p.353.

54. *Singapore Chronicle*, 24 January 1835.

55. The author is grateful to Carl Trocki, a specialist on the Rhio situation in the late eighteenth century, for pointing this out. Gambier is a product used in tanning. It is often cultivated in association with pepper.

56. See Wang, *A Short History of the Nanyang Chinese*, p.19.

57. See V. Purcell, *The Chinese in Malaya* (London, Oxford University Press, 1948), p.70, and P'an, *The Teochews*.

58. *The Penang Register and Miscellany*, 15 September 1821.

59. C. M. Turnbull, *The Straits Settlements 1826-67* (London, Athlone Press, 1972), p.150.

60. Seah, 'The Chinese in Singapore', p.286. Seah's figures were checked with two plantations mentioned in *The Straits Times*, 29 January 1856. Each employed eight people.

61. *Singapore Chronicle*, 11 September 1836.

62. Jackson, *Planters and Speculators*, p.17.

63. See *Straits Settlements Records*, R. F. Wingrove to Murchison, 23 July 1830.

64. Information supplied by Carl Trocki. See also Farquhar's letter of 28 December 1822 in W. Bartley, 'Population of Singapore in 1819', p.177, that to 'various Malays and Chinese the Temenggong has granted leave to clear grounds for plantations about 20 of which commenced before British establishment'.

There is an oral account by a descendant of a Teochew farmer, Chua Chin Huat, opening a gambier settlement near the river, Sungai Berih. This account is found in Agnes Fung Li-Ning, 'Growth of Settlements in Rural Singapore 1819-1957', Academic Exercise for the Geography Department, University of Singapore, 1961/2, p.7.

65. Diary of John Prince, Resident Councillor of Singapore, 2 and 3 July in Straits Settlements Records.

66. It is likely that opium here was sold independently of the British. For example, the *Singapore Free Press* on 24 May 1849 wrote that 'a most extensive arm exists in the jungle for fabricating counterfeiting opium which is sometimes sold to the junks and other native vessels' and urged the opium farmer, he who received the rights from the British, to look out for it.

67. Seah, op. cit., p.286.

68. *Singapore Free Press*, 28 March 1839.

69. The practice of Chinese settlers in Bangkok, when they had any business with a junk was, according to Bowring in 1857, to 'put on board, as supercargo, some relative of their own, generally a young man who has married one of their daughters; the latter take surety of the relatives of the person whom they appoint supercargo. If anything happens to the junk, the individuals who secured her are held responsible.' J. Bowring, *The Kingdom and People of Siam*, Vol. I (London, Parker and Son, 1857). The above reveals that there was a very intimate relationship between the junk people and the people they did business with. Because many of the junks in Singapore would be a spillover from China, there is reason to believe a similar intimate relationship obtained in Singapore. See *Asiatic Journal and Monthly Register*, Vol. 10 (1824-1830) about junks from Siam whose owners 'have been in the habit of doing business (with certain merchants in Singapore)'.

70. See *Singapore Free Press*, 28 March 1839.

71. See *Singapore Free Press*, 28 March 1839; Jackson, *Planters and Speculators*, p.17; Seah, op. cit., p.290.

72. Consider this description in the *Straits Settlements Secret Correspondence*, 14 August 1828 of the junk traffic in coolies. 'On the arrival of the junks opulent Chinese take these labourers off the hands of the commander by paying so much as will redeem them out of power, upon an engagement from the labourers that in consideration of their release, they will work for their benefit for a certain time. Where these poor people retain their health their masters have a reason to be satisfied with their bargains; but where they become sick we have reason to believe that they are often unfeelingly cast off as so much useless lumber.' The 'opulent Chinese' surely could not refer to the pioneers but must rather refer to the financiers. The quotation also suggests from the ease with which the 'opulent Chinese' took the coolies from the commanders of the junk some kind of relationship, as suggested in footnote 69. It is likely then that the pioneer did not obtain his workers direct from the junks but through the Teochew financier, making the financier's stranglehold on the pioneer almost complete. Needless to say, if the money were to be made from the coolie traffic, the financier and the commander of the junk would be the greatest beneficiaries.

73. See *Singapore Free Press*, 28 March 1839.

74. The Europeans did not finance agriculture at this period. We have the word of Fullerton, a high British official in Singapore, in 1830 that it was 'altogether improbable that any portion of the capital now employed by European Settlers in commercial pursuits would for a long time come to be directed to those of agriculture'. Straits Settlements Records; Minutes by the President, 2 March 1830. The Malacca Chinese probably concentrated their energies on the entrepôt, which by 1830 had existed only for some eleven years, a short period for a fortune to be accumulated. Even if they did accumulate some surplus money, by then it is unlikely that they would invest it in such a highly risky endeavour as gambier and pepper agriculture, an agriculture which was also dominated by another dialect group over which they had no control. At any rate, the information we have on the Malacca Chinese shows that, save for Teochews like Seah Eu Chin and Wee Ah Hood who

were assimilated by then, few, if any, made a fortune from gambier and pepper. (Seah Eu Chin was married to a daughter of a Kapitan China in Perak and had contacts with Malacca Chinese. Wee Ah Hood was the son of a Teochew trader who settled in Malacca in 1810.)

Hence the financiers must have been Teochews. At any rate it is clear by the latter half of the century that the bulk of the financiers of this agriculture, according to two knowledgeable observers, were Teochews. See Song, op. cit., p.37 and Li, *A Description*.

III

THE SOCIAL AND POLITICAL ORGANIZATION OF THESE TWO SOCIETIES

THE question raised in this chapter concerns the means that the Malacca Chinese merchants and the Teochew financiers employed to control their respective societies. In other words, without making a prior assumption that they in fact exercised control, what was their relationship with the rest of their societies?

Starting with the entrepôt society, it is necessary to analyse further how the economy operated. The preceding chapter has given what may be called a taxonomy of the class structure. However, this structure, as it actually operated, can be divided into two sectors.

The first includes the further extension of the partnership between the Chinese merchants and the British. It would be logical for the Chinese merchants, as their businesses grew, to be primarily concerned with their relations with the Europeans, from whom the money came, and to allot the business of actually pushing products and collecting produce to other Chinese, who were only too eager to accept. As the preceding classification shows, these petty merchants could either be independent or be employed by the Chinese merchants.

The other sector, here termed for the sake of convenience, the residual economy consisted of those whose existence did not directly derive from the Anglo-Chinese partnership or its extension, but from the overall flourishing of the economy. Its members would be the artisans, those involved in labouring activities, and those members of the petty merchant class whose existence depended upon the people in the residual economy, i.e., those who could market the products of the artisans. These last formed necessarily an extremely small group, because of the pioneer nature of the economy. This residual sector was extremely numerous, far more so than the merchants and their petty followers.[1] As will be seen later, few from this residual economy could even become petty merchants let alone be merchants on the scale of the Malacca Chinese. Moreover, few, if any, could join the small bureaucracy which was the preserve of the Europeans, Singapore then being a colony. What social organizations developed among the Chinese in the entrepôt society?

This question can only be properly understood if the people who came to Singapore are studied. Two aspects of this population are of the greatest relevance here. The first aspect was its unsettled nature. Singapore then was truly a pioneer society, and the men best suited to creating a settlement out of a jungle were likely to be tough and rough. They might not exactly be the wretched of the earth, though there were some analogies,[2] but they would be the adventurous and unfortunate (those Shanghaied, or the captives of wars), probably young and male. Two indications of the unsettled nature of society can be shown. One is the fluidity of the Chinese population, best demonstrated by the phenomenal increase in population over the years. Such an increase could not have been natural.[3]

TABLE II

THE POPULATION OF CHINESE IN SINGAPORE IN VARIOUS YEARS

Year	Numbers of Chinese
1824	3,317
1830	6,555
1836	13,749
1840	17,704
1849	27,988
1860	50,043
1871	54,572
1881	86,766

The other is the scarcity of females, best seen in the high ratio of men to women.[4]

The second aspect was the basic correspondence of the class structure of the entrepôt with divisions among certain dialect groups.[5]

In 1822, Raffles, the founder of Singapore, implied in a letter to European officials on the Island that the more respectable traders were found among the Hokkiens.[6] A government report of the

TABLE III
APPROXIMATE SEX RATIO OF THE CHINESE IN SINGAPORE

Year	Chinese (Males)
1824	8.2
1830	11.3
1836	14.6
1849	11.5
1860	14.4
1871	6.2
1881	5.1

same year is more explicit; all the merchants (probably including merchants and the retailers) were Hokkiens.[7] Probably the most comprehensive list was supplied by Seah Eu Chin in 1848;[8] his compilation, said the knowledgeable British observer, J. D. Vaughan, was a nearly correct account of the different professions and callings of the Chinese.[9] Seah's list shows that the Teochews were petty merchants (the Malacca Chinese were, of course, listed as predominant among the merchants) while the Hakkas and the Cantonese were predominantly artisans. The agriculturalists were mainly Teochews, while the labouring class seems to have been spread out among most of the dialect groups. Some confirmation of Seah's list in 1852 comes from a certain Harry Parkes, an interpreter in Canton, who, in response to questions from his superior officers, answered that the skills of the Hakkas stood them well in the Straits Settlements.[10] He also added that the Teochews were mainly gambier and pepper agriculturists. More than twenty years later in 1876 the knowledgeable British official Pickering, who became the first Protector of the Chinese, wrote that the miners and artisans in the Straits Settlements were mainly Cantonese and Hakkas, while the agriculturists, boatmen, and small shopkeepers were Teochews and Hokkiens.[11] Another British observer, J.D. Vaughan, also observed around 1879 the strong preponderance of Cantonese in the crafts, the Hokkiens among the most wealthy merchants, and the Teochews in gambier and pepper agriculture.[12] Finally, two Chinese officials, as befitting their interest mainly in rich people, wrote, in the later nineteenth century, that the rich merchants were mainly Hokkiens.[13]

Strictly speaking, the sources quoted here reveal a correspondence only between the dialect groups and the occupational structure,

but, from the discussion in our preceding chapter, their relationship to the class structure can be deduced. In the entrepôt economy,
the mercantile class consisted mainly of Hokkiens, including the
Malacca Chinese, while the petty businessmen were also mainly
Hokkiens. Cantonese and Hakkas dominated the crafts, while a
fair mixture of the Cantonese, Hakkas, and Hokkiens, were found
among those not involved in either mercantile pursuits or the crafts.
Those involved in the gambier and pepper economy were primarily
Teochews. Though both Seah and Pickering mentioned that some
Teochews were shopkeepers, it is fairly certain that they were
referring to the Teochew financiers mentioned in the previous
chapter.[14] Beyond the dialect groups referred to here, there was
another group, the Hainanese, mentioned in Seah's list, but they
were mainly domestic servants and comprised an extremely small
percentage of the Chinese population in Singapore. Before turning
to social organization, it may be helpful to describe the places of
origin of these heterogeneous groups. Briefly, the Hokkiens refer
mainly to those Chinese who originated in the area of Fukien,
south of the northern Min speech area and, as far as Singapore
Chinese were then concerned, mainly from the two prefectures of
Chang-chou and Chuan-chou. The term 'Hokkien' is the pronunciation in this dialect of the province of Fukien though sometimes the term 'Chinchew' is also used.[15] ('Chinchew' is the pronunciation, again in that dialect, of the prefecture of Chang-chou.)
The Teochews, though their dialect has some similarity to the
Hokkiens, nevertheless originated in the prefecture of Chao-chou,
particularly from eight of the ten districts within it near the Fukien
border.[16] The Hakkas, originally migrants from the north of China,
were quite scattered. Strong concentrations could be found in the
prefecture of Chia-ying chou and the other two districts of Chao-
chou prefecture while lesser concentrations were found in some of
the other eight districts of Chao-chou and in parts of Fukien and
Kwangtung.[17] They speak a dialect more akin to Mandarin than
the other four dialects. South-west of Kwangtung in the Pearl
River Delta are seven districts where the Cantonese originated.
Sometimes these Cantonese were referred to as Macaos, particularly before the opening of Hong Kong in 1842, for then the
Cantonese embarked overseas through the port of Macao.[18] While
the term Hainanese literally means the inhabitants of Hainan, the
bulk of those in Singapore came from two districts, Wen-chang and
Chung-shan in the north-eastern part of the island.

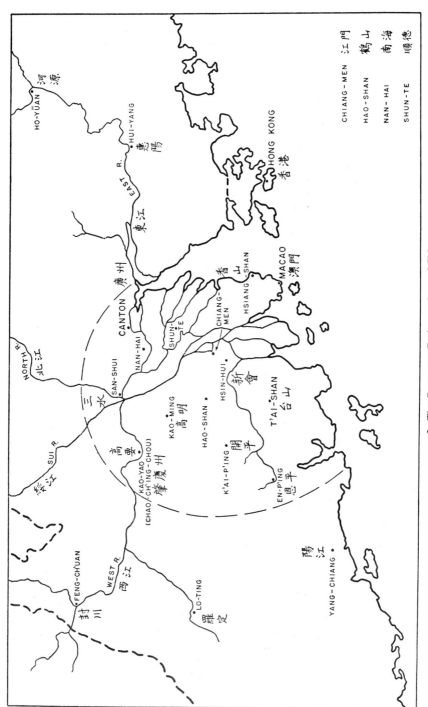

2. The Cantonese Emigrant Area of China

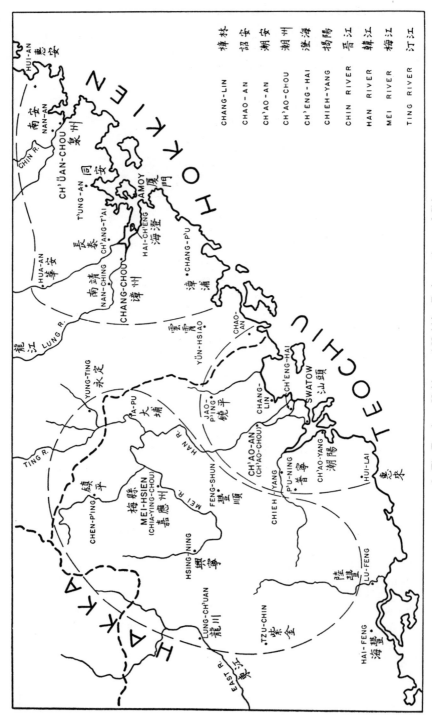

3. The Teochew, Hakka, and Hokkien Emigrant Areas of China

樺林	韶安	湖安	湖州	澄海	揭陽	晉江	韓江	梅江	汀江
CHANG-LIN	CHAO-AN	CH'AO-AN	CH'AO-CHOU	CH'ENG-HAI	CHIEH-YANG	CHIN RIVER	HAN RIVER	MEI RIVER	TING RIVER

As both the fluidity and the dialect group/class correspondence in Chinese society in Singapore had consequences for social organization, they will be further discussed in this context. In general, there was a basic coincidence between those who spoke a particular dialect and a certain territory. Now, in China, it is known that social organizations were traditionally formed on the basis of a common territorial origin. One of the most important kinds was the *hui-kuan*, an association of fellow-provincials in some other part of China on official duty or on business.[19] There were many reasons why fellow-provincials should associate. The merchants needed official protection, while the officials could benefit from certain financial arrangements the merchants might deem it wise to make. There were also sentimental attachments.

A second basis of social organization in China, much tighter in fact, rested on a coincidence between blood and territory, the resulting organization being variously termed sub-clan or lineage. Maurice Freedman has shown how pervasive this lineage structure was in south-eastern China whence our migrants came.[20] Agnatic descendants formed a village or a group of villages and the manifestations of their cohesion ranged from lineages being associated with one particular village or a few close villages, to many disparate villages maintaining their unity only by keeping a common estate.

There was still another basis of organization—real or presumed blood-ties, again agnatically defined. Chinese having the same surname, though they might be from different areas in China, could organize on the grounds that in the distant past they had a common ancestor. The term 'clan' seems an appropriate term for this kind of organization.

Now the situation in early Singapore was such that it was unlikely that there would be many immigrants agnatically related who also hailed from a village or villages close to one another (in other words, from the same lineage). For one thing, before 1820 there was a Manchu ban on emigration.[21] While this may have been flouted, it must have had some effect in restraining lineages from encouraging their members to migrate. Those who slipped through the net were mainly those who were either involuntary captives of press-gangs, or criminals and adventurers, characters, who, in any number, would be spread over quite a wide area of China. Nor were the lineages themselves over-eager to emigrate. This can be seen from the fact that prior to 1893 lineage councils did not encourage

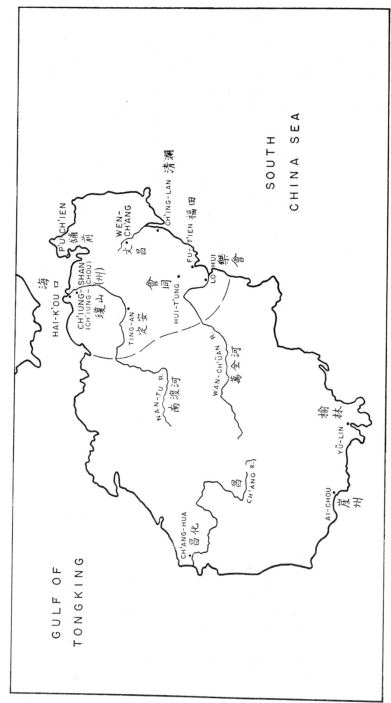

海口 HAI-K'OU
海

GULF OF
TONGKING

CH'IUNG-SHAN
(CH'IUNG-CHOU) 瓊山(州)
PU'CH'IEN 舖前
WEN-CH'ANG 文昌
CH'ING-LAN 清瀾
FU-T'IEN 福田
TING-AN 定安
HUI-T'UNG 會同
LO-HUI 樂會

NAN-T'U R. 南渡河
WAN-CH'UAN R. 萬全河

YÜ-LIN 榆林

CH'ANG R. 昌江

CHANG-HUA 昌化

AI-CHOU 崖州

SOUTH
CHINA SEA

4. The Hainanese Emigrant Area of China

wives to accompany their husbands for fear of losing the family along with the man.[22] While what was sauce for the goose might not necessarily be sauce for the gander, it is unlikely that the lineage councils encouraged the men to emigrate either. At any rate, a well-known Chinese merchant, testifying before a government commission on labour as late as 1876, said he knew, generally, of no labourers who came to Singapore from villages very close to each other or had the same surname.[23]

Thus, the one basis left for solidarity in Singapore was a common territorial origin or a common dialect.[24] That was the basis on which the Malacca Chinese identified with the Hokkiens. They could do so, despite long years of domicile in the Malay Peninsula, because their ancestors originated in southern Fukien. That they did so seems clear from the record. First, contemporary accounts lumped them together. A government report of 1822 described the merchants, many of whom were Malacca Chinese, as Hokkiens.[25] The missionary Stronach wrote in his diary that he had conversations with many Hokkiens but revealed later on in the same diary that many of these Hokkiens were in fact Malacca Chinese.[26] That he seems to have used these two terms interchangeably makes a strong case for seeing both as one. After all, a European would find it easy to distinguish the Malacca Chinese, because they were Westernized from other Chinese. Not doing so clearly suggests some identity between the two groups. But the most compelling evidence can be found in the Hokkien temple, mentioned in the previous chapter. It was then the organization *par excellence* of the Hokkiens and the Malacca Chinese were not only Hokkiens in the eyes of the Hokkien community but also comprised the group's leadership.

In what ways did a common dialect contribute to solidarity? It is useful here to make an analytical distinction between the fact of people of the same dialect group being in one place, and its organizational expression, though in practice the latter was a function of the former.

The average migrant arrived in Singapore without friend or family. This meant that he had to seek aid from others, assuming that others did not first seek him out. The fact that the others were all Chinese was not of great importance. Chinese nationalism then did not exist, and, moreover, back in China, he related only to his kinsmen in his village or in villages close by. In the absence of such kinsmen, he would then seek people who spoke his dialect and soon a bond of solidarity would arise. This tendency was strengthened by his inability to communicate with people of other dialect groups. For example, a Hakka could not communicate with a Hainanese except in Mandarin (not in wide use then in China and confined mainly to officials), or in written Chinese (the bulk of the immigrants were illiterate).[27] Moreover, between some dialect groups there was a long history of hostility, if not actual conflict. The Hakkas and the Cantonese had long felt hostile to each other in China and wars between them had actually erupted at this period. It seems logical then that barring outside intervention solidarity should arise on a dialect group basis.

The solidarity arising from common dialect origin was probably one factor contributing to trust between the Chinese merchants and the petty merchants in the entrepôt economy. As stated, both groups were primarily Hokkiens. From the perspective of the merchants, it would be safer to entrust cash or goods on credit to petty merchants who were also Hokkiens. These petty merchants would try to be worthy of this trust, since it allowed them to stay in business, not to mention other benefits which might possibly arise from association with the rich and powerful. A not unimportant contributory factor was the small number of these petty merchants; the Malacca Chinese would want to employ the smallest number convenient in order to reduce the element of risk.

In the Singapore of our period, there were different organizational expressions of the dialect groups. For example, in the case of the Hokkiens, they first began organizing, as mentioned previously, with the construction of a temple and later on with a *hui-kuan*.[28] It is more illuminating however to view institutions such as the temple and the *hui-kuan* in the Singapore context as two ends of a continuum, the temple having functions catering to the most basic needs of men such as a decent burial and minimal assistance[29] in difficult times, while the *hui-kuan* had more sophisticated functions such as the support of education[30] and cultural activities, the search for employment, and even political action.[31] Both were used by the Malacca Chinese to gain 'legitimacy' in Hokkien eyes, especially among the many Hokkiens who were not petty merchants and who did not have direct economic ties with them.

Apart from the prestige arising from their association with officialdom (the British administration clearly favoured them) the Malacca Chinese had to do 'good works' in order to gain recognition from the Hokkien community for their leadership. Some evidence of this can be seen in Tan Tock Seng's conversation with Stronach

that he contributed much money to the Hokkien temple, despite
the fact that he did not believe in idols, because there was pressure
from the Hokkiens on the rich merchants to build a place of wor-
ship.[32] Beyond this, what other 'good works' were necessary?
Not many. Because of the fluid and unsettled nature of society,
demands beyond those catered to by the temple were few. As there
were few families, little pressure was exerted on dialect group leaders for facilities such as schools, cultural, and other associations,
as normally found in more settled populations. It is not surprising then that the main public organizational expression of the
Hokkiens in the first half of the nineteenth century was the
temple.

The performance of good works, channelled primarily through
the temple, did not give the Malacca Chinese full control over even
the Hokkiens, let alone the free trade population as a whole. For
that, force was needed. The Malacca Chinese basically had none,
except that of the European state, which taxed them but was not
much bothered about governing the Chinese for most of the
nineteenth century. In this connexion, the secret societies played
an important role. Secret societies, or those designated in the
accounts as such, existed as many separate organizations in Singapore.[33] There has been some controversy as to whether they did
actually all originate from one parent society or from two. The
father of the theory of the two parents was M. L. Wynne who
argued that they were the Triad Society (variously called the
Three Dot Society, the Heaven and Earth League, and the Hung
League) and the Ko-lao-Hui or the Han League.[34] Among the
more important opponents of this theory was W. L. Blythe who
believed that there was only one.[35] It would seem Blythe has the
better of the argument.[36] Moreover, as far as Singapore is concerned, there is no disagreement that the Triad fathered the most
societies. More relevant to our discussion is the structure of these
societies, which does not seem to have varied much, regardless
of origin.

It is not certain whether the various secret societies in Singapore
then were all different branches of the parent Triad in China
(assuming a single origin) or whether they emanated from one
branch of the Triad which first came to Singapore. It is also possible that there were other branches elsewhere in South-East Asia.[37]
But it is clear that, for a time, a central organization or council
existed, which contained representatives of all the various dialect

groups.[38] It is likely that branches or lodges radiated from this central organization. It is also clear that the leadership of each lodge was vested in three brothers, all sworn and not blood.[39]

While the secret societies may have had some religious attributes, 'brotherhood' was what they were all about. This featured in the legendary origin of the societies in China in the second century A.D. Three strangers, Liu Pei, Kuan Yu, and Chang Fei, met in a peach garden and bound themselves under an oath of brotherhood to be loyal to each other until death, to save the threatened state and to serve the people. When the Triad Society was formed very much later by Ming Loyalists to fight the Manchus, the society retained the same brotherhood myth of origin.[40]

As far as can be seen, this was the ideological framework the secret societies imposed on the Chinese in Singapore. From all accounts, these societies, if they did not dominate the entire Chinese population, certainly controlled the population of the residual economy. Thus, a Chinese, who had spent many years in the Straits Settlements, wrote in 1833 that secret societies 'have risen up in all the Settlements'.[41] Figures are supplied many years later. 'I am not overstating facts,' wrote Pickering (who was one to know) in 1876, 'when I say that over 60% of the Chinese population in our colonies and the native states are sworn members of the secret societies and of the remaining 40% most are subject to their influences.'[42] Another independent and knowledgeable observer, J. D. Vaughan, giving a slightly smaller but nevertheless still high percentage, estimated that 40,000 Chinese belonged to the secret societies in 1879.[43] The Chinese population in 1881, according to the census, amounted to 86,766. By the late 1880s there was general acknowledgement in the European community that the secret societies controlled the Chinese population. The force of this acknowledgement was brought out in a question by members of the European-dominated legislative council in 1889 to the Governor, who intended to ban them, as to whether the time had come 'when our police force and the protectorate are able to control the mass of Chinese in Singapore'.[44] Hitherto the secret societies had been presumed to be in control.

The secret society domination of the population of the residual economy can best be explained by comparing them with the dialect associations and the clans; and three aspects can be fruitfully considered.

First, the secret societies were able to generate a sense of brotherhood among the Chinese of different dialect groups and clans. They were, in fact, of a different genre from the 'natural' organizations of clans and dialect associations. In Chesneaux's words, they were 'not founded on the acceptance of the natural condition of man, as were the family, the clan and the village, and the guild but on voluntary initiative'.[45] Now the Singapore Chinese population then might not be exactly 'unnatural', but because the only other important social organizations were the dialect associations and the clans, which perforce were limited in the people from which membership could be drawn, the secret societies had a clear field. The dialect associations themselves could unite, as they did later under the chambers of commerce, but this was not in the offing in early nineteenth century Singapore.

Moreover, the secret societies themselves possessed a ritualistic mechanism which was quite effective in reinforcing this sense of brotherhood. One of the highlights of the initiation was the forcing of a new member to drink the blood of some older members to symbolize their new-found brotherhood. He also was enjoined to obey the secret society elders as he would his own parents (in fact, he had first to renounce his actual parents if they were alive) and swear oaths of loyalty to secret society laws. Threats were used, and some flavour of this can be gleaned from a look at the first article of the two rival societies then in existence in Singapore, the Triad society and the Ghee Hok, presumed by Wynne to have sprung from the Han League. The first article of the Triad states:

> From the moment that you have entered the Hung League you must quietly fulfill your duties, and keep to your own business. It has always been said that filial love is the first of all virtues; therefore, you must respect and obey both your parents, and obey and venerate your superiors. Do not resist your father and mother and, so, violate the laws of the Hung League. He who does not keep this command, most surely, will not be suffered by Heaven and Earth, but he shall be crushed by five thunderbolts! Each of you ought to obey this.

That of the Ghee Hok adds punishment for violators in most graphic terms:

> After entering the Hong Gate (the Ghee Hok), a member of the Hong family must above all things obey and honour his parents, he must also abstain from injuring the parents of a brother Hong. If he breaks this oath may he within 100 days die by being cut to pieces, or in the five seas, his flesh floating on the surface, and his bones sinking to the bottom.[46]

This surely must have had a strong effect on the Chinese population. From two different perspectives, then, we find some substantiation for our assertions. A European observer, impressed but negative, wrote in 1849 that it is probable

> ... the inventors of the oaths and the initiatory rites by which mutual safety is assured, have carefully appealed to every natural and superstitious fear that has a place in the Chinese breast, and have bound the members to inviolable secrecy and fidelity by denunciations of certain vengeances in this world and every torment and evil after death to which in their belief man can be doomed.[47]

On the other hand, the secret societies themselves (as translated in the *Singapore Free Press*, some ungrammatically and thus corrected in this quotation) stated that they were invited by Tan Che Sang in the early days to come to Singapore because Tan 'in the knowledge which he undoubtedly possessed of the peculiar characteristics of his countrymen [chose the secret societies] because [they were] then the best managed associations, with imposing ceremonials, and the largest sphere of action'.[48]

The sense of brotherhood was further strengthened by the ability of the secret societies to use force to ensure that the member who wavered in his belief would think twice about deserting the society. Munshi Abdullah wrote of the secret societies' readiness to use force when they executed one who refused to join; there were many other cases of force used on members who broke the laws of the secret societies.[49] That the secret societies were not without arms is clear. The same Munshi Abdullah also wrote that he saw in a secret society hideout 'ten large shields, 3 iron tridents, about 20 short swords, 6 or 7 swords . . . [and] a great many muskets leaning against the wall'.[50] Quite apart from the fact that force anywhere has a value of its own, in Singapore it was all the more impressive since other institutions, such as the clans and the dialect group associations, had little or none.[51]

Finally, the secret societies could take care of their members; they had a real social value. We do not mean merely 'welfare assistance', such as aid in times of sickness, indigence, and woe. If that were the case, they would have been no different from the dialect associations and the clans. They were also able to organize their members to oppose unjust governmental action, though not always successfully, and for justice in work arrangements. As examples of the former, we can mention the 1851 and 1857 incidents, to be discussed in the next chapter, while of the latter, a European observer wrote that secret societies in the plantations organized the workers to accept lower wages, in times of difficulty, so as to prevent unemployment.[52]

We may ask further, what was there that called for the special methods of the secret societies? The answer is first, the extraordinary nature of the population with its lack of families. The secret societies acted as a kind of parental substitute. The second is an extraordinary situation in the sense of a harsh and·hostile environment, and a government, if not hostile, at best indifferent. Hence, force and a strong organization were needed to create effective social ties.

It remains to inquire whether the merchant class controlled the population of the residual economy by controlling the secret societies. There were speculations and rumours in the early years that some merchants were members of or contributed money to the secret societies. Some might have been members but it is clear that, as a class, they were not. As early as 1831, the then superintendent of police, Bonham, in a study of the secret societies, claimed that the respectable Malacca Chinese were not members.[53] In 1874, the *Singapore Daily Times* wrote that the opinion of the Europeans generally was that the respectable Chinese were not members but, in fact, wanted the government to take action against them.[54] Finally, no less an authority than Pickering claimed that the respectable Chinese were not members. 'Nay,' he said, 'the opinion of every respectable Chinese in the Straits Settlements is that the recognition of the Hoeys, or Heaven and Earth Society [secret societies], is a disgrace to our government.'[55] Here, respectable Chinese meant the merchants.

Such statements were confirmed by the behaviour of the most prominent merchants who, at times of rioting, supposedly organized by the secret societies, did all they could to help the government to restore order.[56] That would not be the case if they were the leaders of the secret societies.

An examination of the leadership of the secret societies tells the same story. Here are the names (dictated simply by their availability in the documents) of those associated with the secret societies before 1846, those which came under the first published schedule of Chinese secret societies in Singapore in 1877, and those which came under the last published schedule of Chinese secret societies in Singapore before proscription in 1890 will be examined to see if any merchants were included. (Other lists were published after 1877 but these three are sufficient for our purpose.)

Names of Secret Society Leaders found by the author before 1846

Ho Yem Ko	Founder and President of the Triad Society; 1846.
Ho Ah Yam	Another Founder; 1819.
Tan Tek Hye	Keeper of the Quinquanguler Seal, Singapore Secret Society Temple; 1846.[57]
Ayun Ko	Head of Triad Society; 1830.
Tan Yin Gwan	Another Head; 1830.
Ahun-Teo	Head of Keh Tribe Fraternity; 1830.[58]

These names were compared with the list of the merchants found in the *Straits Directory* before 1850 and with a list of merchants who made a petition to the government in 1841. None of the six were found in either.[59]

The 1877 list contains the following:[60]

Name of Society	Name of Society President	Occupation
Ghee Hin (Hokkien)	Cho Kim Siang	Coolie Broker
Ghee Hin (Teochew)	Teo Ah Koah	Gambier Shopkeeper
Ghee Hin (Hylam)	Ong Chee Teck	Sawyer
Ghee Hok	Chua Moh Choon	Doctor and Theatre Manager
Ghee Sin	Tan Soon Qwan	Opium Shopkeeper
Ghee Khee	Chong Chok Chong	Goldsmith
Kong Hok		
Kok Kin	Tan Ong Leang	No Occupation
Kong Hooy Lew	Hoo Ah Tuk	Independent
Song Peh	Leong Ah Pan	Sawyer
Hai San	Seah Kiat Sing	Geomancer

Some are listed here as shopkeepers. But they were petty merchants, for the list has been checked with a list of Chinese merchants in the *Straits Directory* and none corresponded.[61] The 1890 list, taken from the same source as the 1877 list, contains the following names (see p.53).

This list was checked with names of Chinese merchants found in the *Straits Directory* in the years from 1880 to 1900 and again none corresponded.

Name of Society	Name of Society President	Occupation
Ghee Hin (Hokkien)	Gan Kam Lian	Druggist
Ghee Hok	Ang Ah Hiang	Coffinmaker
Ghee Khee Kwang Hok	Liun Mah Tek	Gambier Shopkeeper
Hok Kin	Poh Kim Thak	Opium Shopkeeper
Kwang Fui Sin	Wang Ah Si	Carpenter
Song Peh Kwang	Khew Choe	Sawyer
Hong Ghee Tong	Cheang Ah Hong	Spirit Shopkeeper
Lee Seng Hong	Yang Ah Lam	Carpenter
Yet Tong Kun	Ng Yaw Seng	Shoemaker
Heng Sim	Lau Kim	Cargo Boatman

Such a situation on analysis is not surprising. For, on a cultural level, the Malacca Chinese were the most de-sinicized of all the immigrant groups. The symbolism of the secret societies was taken from Chinese mythology, and if one way of controlling a society is by the manipulation of symbols, then the Malacca Chinese would probably perform poorly compared to the others. Or, if they had controlled the secret societies, they would probably have had to alter the symbolism or change it to something they could manage, something more appropriate to the local situation.

Moreover, they could not even partake of the symbolism, being neither culturally nor residentially in harmony with the rest of the membership. Thus, the *Singapore Chronicle* in 1831 commented:

We must have observed that the descendants of Chinese or those not born in China are never permitted to become members [of the Triad Society], either because the Chinese consider them an inferior race, or they are unwilling to entrust them with secrets, lest in some crucial instances their natural connection with the country they reside in should produce a betrayal.[62]

Moreover the manner by which success in business came about consisted of ingratiating oneself with the Europeans, as distinct from the manner necessary in the residual economy, where most of the money was made from kidnapping coolies, from prostitution, and crime. It is conceivable that those who succeeded in the residual economy used the secret societies to do so; while those in the top structure had a professional interest in disavowing or playing down any connexions they might have with the secret societies, simply because the Europeans frowned on them as is indicated by the many pages of invective against their alleged criminal nature.

Lacking direct control, then, the Malacca Chinese sought protection from the state. The resulting alliance can be readily seen. Because Singapore was a colonial society where political power and the bureaucracy were denied to the Chinese, the state's favour was expressed by making the Malacca Chinese unofficial administrators of the Chinese community—as unofficial Kapitans China and as Justices of the Peace—and by conferring social prestige on them. The former trend can be seen by examining the Kapitans China, whom the British considered as leaders of Chinese society. The Kapitans China had official status before 1826, because then there were no legally constituted courts of law, but their status was made unofficial when a new charter was granted to the Company for Singapore by the British Parliament. In 1873, W. H. Read,[63] then a legislative council member, stated that there had been three Kapitans China so far, and they were:

Tan Tock Seng — merchant
Tan Kim Seng — merchant
Tan Kim Ching — merchant

Further, the British did much to elevate their social prestige. Raffles himself considered the mercantile profession to be the most respectable, and the policy of subsequent governments was to invite mainly merchants to state occasions, and to consult with them over matters affecting the Chinese community. An examination of the *Straits Directory* from 1866 to 1872, which lists those who the European community thought were the principal inhabitants of the country, is enlightening. Their occupations are obtained from other sources.

Tan Tock Sing	merchant
Whampoa or Hoo Ah Kay	merchant
Hooding	merchant
(Tan) Kim Seng	merchant
(Tan) Koh Teow	Kim Seng's partner
Kuchan	merchant
Lim Sim Chai	merchant
Lee Tek Soo	no information
See Eng Watt	merchant
See Koh Guan	merchant
See Kown Guan	merchant
See Moh Guan	merchant
Tan Beng Swee	merchant
Tan Sue Lim	partner Kim Seng
Tan Kim Swee	partner Kim Seng

Sin Book Whatt	no information
Seah Eu Chin	merchant
See Boon Siang	no information
Lim Thean Giow	assistant to an opium farmer
	Cheang Hong Lim
Tan Seng Poh	merchant, brother-in-law of
	Seah Eu Chin

While the state did not actually intervene in the regulation of the population of the residual economy till around the 1870s it nevertheless had stationed in Singapore a military force that was meant to be, and actually was, used to prevent riots as is easily seen from the statements of responsible officials. Three such will suffice. In the secret correspondence of the *Straits Settlements Records* in 1827, the Resident Councillor, in reply to a query from the Governor about a reduction of troops, said that because of the turbulent Singapore population it was not wise 'to dispense with any portion of the troops now employed'.[64] Sir William Norris, Recorder, addressed the Grand Jury in 1837 with regard to Chinese in the interior of Singapore saying that if the civil powers were insufficient to pacify the Chinese population there, 'the military should be called in to assist'.[65] In 1856-7, the European community protested against the conveyance of a small military force to Hong Kong on the grounds that it would be impolitic to weaken the military forces when the Chinese population appeared so volatile.[66] In the two violent years of 1854 and 1857 the military was actually used to pacify the Chinese population. That the purpose of such a force was to police the entrepôt society can not have been lost on the secret societies, and hence the population of the residual economy was restrained.

Regarding the gambier and pepper society, the Teochew financiers faced essentially two problems in maintaining their control. The first was to ensure the good faith of the pioneer, given a situation where the state, English or native, hardly intervened; the second was to obtain the acquiescence of the workers. We can usefully distinguish here between two kinds of situation: a 'normal' situation and an 'extraordinary' situation. The latter refers to a situation of depression in the prices of the two crops and the incursion of hostile forces.

Under normal conditions, the system worked smoothly enough. The pioneer, like any other migrant, cherished the idea of making good, and hence would try to make the system work. Second,

even if he wanted to abscond, it might not be worth it. The financier did not give the advance all at once, but only a small amount at a time.[67] By the time the pioneer had gathered a large sum, he would have already, through great effort, gone a long way towards creating a plantation. Here, the observation by a newspaper of the Penang situation no doubt also applied to Singapore. Even if the planter were of a roguish disposition, the *Free Press* wrote, he 'is as it were bound over to good behaviour by the interest which he has acquired in his plantation and the trusts of which he would run the risk of forfeiting by a serious infringement of the laws'.[68] Finally, the pioneer was dependent on the financier not only for cash but for basic provisions such as rice, clothes, etc. He was different from the peasant turned commercial agricultural worker who could always return to his home village for a bare subsistence should he be disenchanted. The home village of the pioneer was in China, and he could not expect to make the dash home very easily. The surrounding local environment, peopled as it was by non-Chinese, would be at best indifferent to his fate.

For their part, the workers would acquiesce in the system for all the above reasons except for the second; they had less of a share because they did not own any plantations. The workers were of two kinds: those indentured for a year to the pioneer or financier and those who were free and worked primarily for wages. 'Free' workers largely continued as such probably because they could not obtain advances from the financiers to start plantations of their own. Their acquiescence in their condition may have been heightened by opium smoking and the power of the secret societies.

The secret societies have hitherto been discussed primarily in the urban context. There are accounts, however, which show that they existed in the gambier and pepper society. Munshi Abdullah wrote of a trip to a secret society hideout in the interior of Singapore in 1824,[69] while Bonham, in 1831,[70] wrote that some planters were recruited to the secret societies voluntarily while some were compelled forcibly by threats of having their plantations burned or themselves being driven out. Contemporary newspapers too attest to their existence.[71]

Were the secret societies used to maintain existing social arrangements? James Jackson speculated that the economic hierarchy of the gambier and pepper society probably coincided with the hierarchy of the secret societies.[72] If this were the case, the leaders of the secret societies would probably have been the financiers

and the successful pioneers while the rest would consist of workers and less successful pioneers. Such a structure probably did obtain when there was no crisis though less markedly than suggested by Jackson. The rich would have both the means and the interest to hire toughs to ensure that the workers did not get out of line. On the other hand, there was clearly a real sense of brotherhood, derived from the fact that the agriculturists and financiers were primarily of one dialect group, the Teochews. The rural secret society leaders would thus have more promising material to work with than their urban counterparts who had to weld a mass of people from different dialect groups into believing in the brotherly bond.

The question arises, nevertheless, of why, if the agriculturists were primarily Teochews, did dialect group associations not arise, as happened among the Hokkiens in the town? Two reasons may be advanced. First, there were few families in the interior. A Dutch account of a gambier and pepper society in Rhio revealed that beyond a few prostitutes for the financiers, there were no females.[73] Things were evidently not very different in Singapore, judging from Seah's account of the Chinese mentioned previously.

Moreover, it was an extremely harsh environment, particularly for the workers, and the coercive element had to be that much stronger. In the town, as far as the Hokkiens were concerned, it did not suit the interests of the Malacca Chinese to create coercive organizations, quite apart from the fact that they were unable to do so. They were not needed to control the petty merchants. (It was more important for both to put their heads together to get a good deal from the natives than for the Malacca Chinese to ensure the subservience of the petty merchants.) And as for the other Hokkiens, why bother? If they proved troublesome, the British military could always be called in. In the interior, however, the financiers had to make the workers work, and coercive organizations were an essential tool.[74]

Could the financiers and the successful pioneers control the secret societies in extraordinary situations, given that they constituted a very small minority of the membership? The evidence is that they could not. For example, in 1831 when the prices of gambier and pepper were very low, the *Singapore Chronicle* wrote that the secret societies went around disrupting the plantations that did not belong to them.[75] There were also accounts of secret societies leading people from the interior to attack the people in the town.[76] These reports suggest that as the financiers became more and more removed from the agriculture by moving into the town, secret societies began to be captured by the unsuccessful pioneers and workers. This separation of financiers and unsuccessful pioneers and workers was greatly accentuated by free trade. This is one of the main considerations of the next chapter, which analyses the social convulsions caused when the entrepôt society intruded into the gambier and pepper society.

1. See figures supplied by Seah, 'The Chinese'.
2. See *Straits Settlements Secret Correspondence*, 2 November 1828; *Singapore Chronicle*, 1 July 1830.
3. Taken from Saw Swee Hock, *Singapore Population in Transition* (Philadelphia, University of Pennsylvania Press, 1970), p.57.
4. Calculated from Saw, op. cit., p.60.
5. The immigrants from China were divided in many ways, but these divisions have been mainly identified linguistically in scholarly literature. Out of the many groups who spoke different dialects in the three provinces of Kwangtung, Fukien, and Hainan, only five will be identified as they were the most important within the context of Chinese society in Singapore. They were the groups which spoke Hokkien, Teochew, Hakka, Cantonese, and Hainanese.

The official British practice was to call these groups 'tribes' (see official British Censuses of Malaya and Singapore, e.g., 1921 and 1931). Maurice Freedman rightly suggested that a more unsuitable word was difficult to imagine. See his 'Kinship, Local Organization and Migration: a study in social realignment among Chinese overseas' (Ph.D. thesis, University of London, 1956). As Skinner said, the term is particularly inapt since 'both the technical and anthropological sense and the popular meaning are scarcely germane'. (See his *Chinese Society in Thailand*, Cornell University Press, 1957, p.35.) Nor is the term 'congregation', used by the French in Indochina appropriate, for it implies a formal organization. Now while these dialect groups did have formal organizations, particularly in the latter part of the nineteenth century, the term 'congregation' is too restrictive as it can exclude those who were not members of a formal organization. Certainly it is not appropriate for the fluid society of our period where formal organization on dialect group lines was not pervasive. Skinner himself preferred the term 'speech group' because it was the most 'accurate so far as it goes and otherwise non-committal'. He argued that the term 'dialect' suggested something like a variance from the standard language but nevertheless intelligible to the speakers of that standard language, very much like speakers of the southern dialect in America are intelligible to those who speak, if there is such a thing, standard American; and vice versa. Not so with the dialect groups here. While they were all dialects of Chinese, only in the written ideographic script were they united. Before the May Fourth Movement of 1919 when the written vernacular (Chinese written as it is spoken by the people) was introduced as a popular medium of writing, Chinese was written in the classical style, *wen-yan* and could only be comprehended by the people with many years of schooling in the classical style. Such literacy in the written Chinese language did not obtain with a majority of the Chinese in Singapore. Worse, even if some were literate, it had to be in the classical style, as the written vernacular had then not been introduced. Otherwise, spoken Hainanese, for example, was unintelligible to speakers of Cantonese or Hakka, and vice versa.

Skinner, of course, is technically correct, but the term 'speech group' does not, as Skinner himself probably would agree, bring out the full force of the divisions within these migrants, divisions which have added territorial and socio-economic dimensions. As examples of the former, the Hakkas from the two districts Ta-pu and Feng-shun, of the prefecture of Chao-chou sometimes joined in the activities, such as religious ceremonies and the organizational structure of the Teochews from the other eight districts, on the grounds that both groups were from Chao-chou. Conversely, common 'speech group' members could split, among other grounds, on the fact that they were from different territories. That happened with the Hakkas from the prefecture of Hwei-chou and the Hakkas from Chia-ying-chou who fought each other in the nineteenth century on the Malay Peninsula. Examples of the latter were people from northern Fukien, who were speakers of a different 'speech' from the Hokkiens, but who desired to join with the Hokkiens because the latter were much wealthier in the nineteenth century; some Hakkas, in the twentieth century, expressed a similar desire to join with the Hokkiens, again because the Hokkiens were wealthy. Hence, the term 'dialect group', despite its imperfection, has its uses.

6. Song, *One Hundred Years*, p.12.

7. *Journal of the Indian Archipelago*, Vol. LX, 1855, see section 'Notices of Singapore', p.468.

8. Seah, op. cit., p.290.

9. 'Notes on the Chinese in the Straits', *Journal of the Indian Archipelago*, Vol. LX, 1855, p.116.

10. In answers to queries from the Earl of Malmesbury through Dr. Bowring in correspondence with the Superintendent of British Trade in China over the subject of immigration from China. Such found in *British Parliamentary Papers*, Cmd., 1866, Enclosure No. 10.

11. W. A. Pickering, 'The Chinese in the Straits of Malacca', *Fraser's Magazine* (London, October 1876), p.440.

12. Vaughan, *Manners and Customs*, p.15.

13. By a Chinese minister to Great Britain, Hsieh Fu-Ching, in a memorial to the Emperor quoted in Chen Ta, *Emigrant Communities in South China* (New York, Secretariat, Institute of Pacific Relations, 1940), p.54, and Li, *A Description of Singapore*, p.9.

14. Another way to show that the agriculturists were primarily Teochews would be the migration figures later in the nineteenth century (*Straits Settlements Censuses of 1881, 1891,* and *1901*). By then Singapore was primarily an urban society, and in these years the population figures for Hokkiens and Cantonese increased dramatically while the Teochew figures were not so impressive. This confirms the urban nature of Cantonese and Hokkien pursuits.

15. See Chang Li-ch'ien, *Ma-lu-chia shih* (*A History of Malacca*), Singapore, 1941, and *Singapore Free Press*, 28 September 1849.

16. The eight districts are Chao-an, Cheng-hai, Chieh-yang, Jao-ping, Pu-ning, Chao-yang, Hui-lai, and Nan-on. According to Skinner, op. cit., p.37, the bulk of the Teochew immigrants was concentrated in the first six districts. But in 1962 there were apparently quite a lot of Teochew immigrants from the other two districts, enough for the Teochews in Malaysia and Singapore to form an association of Teochews from the eight districts. Hence, Malaysia and Singapore drew mainly from eight rather than six districts. The other two districts of the prefecture of Chao-chou, Feng-shun and Ta-pu have large concentrations of Hakkas.

17. Some are found in Chieh-yang, for example, and also in the district of Yung-ting prefecture in Kwangtung. As to the history of the Hakkas, there is an interesting personal account by Han Suyin, whose mother was Flemish and father a Hakka from the province of Szechuan, in *The Crippled Tree* (New York, Putnam, 1965).

18. The seven districts are Hsin-hui, T'ai-shan, En-p'ing, K'ai-ping, Nan-hai, Pan-yu and Shun-te. As to the Macao label, see Seah, op. cit., p.290.

For the convenience of the reader, three maps showing the places of origins of the immigrants are appended. They are taken from Skinner, *Chinese Society.*

19. See H. B. Morse, *The Gilds of China with an Account of the Gild Merchant or Co-Hong of Canton* (Shanghai, Hong Kong, Singapore, Kelly and Walsh, Ltd. 2nd edition, 1932), p.61.

20. Maurice Freedman, *Lineage Organization in Southeastern China* (London, The Athlone Press, 1970), p.1. The lineage is sometimes called a sub-clan. See T'ien, *The Chinese*, p.23.

21. The Manchus during most of the dynasty did not permit emigration for fear that the emigrants, once out of reach, would turn anti-Manchu and plot against them. Some of the resistance against the Manchus in the early years of their dynasty came from Chinese who fled to the island of Taiwan. But their law against migration was never effectively enforced against the adventurous and those made desperate by tremendous economic hardships. The Western powers, in need of Chinese migrants for their colonies, forced the Manchus to relax the law in 1860, and by 1889 it was actually repealed. See Victor Purcell, *The Chinese in Southeast Asia* (Oxford, Oxford University Press, 2nd edition, 1966), pp.26-7.

22. Skinner, op. cit., p.126.

23. Testimony of Tan Seng Poh before a commission on labour. See 'The Report of Committee Appointed to consider and take Evidence upon the Conditions of Chinese Labourers in the Straits Settlements 1876' in the records of the Colonial Office 275/19.

As further evidence, a list of nineteen coolies who received advances from a European company based in Singapore for work in Deli, Sumatra, is reproduced. It is taken from 'The Report'. While there is no way of judging if they, or a majority of them, were from one particular village or dialect group, at least it shows that they were not members of a lineage or a clan, given the different surnames of so many.

Names of Coolies

Wee Ah Kow	Tan Heng
Kway Yee Hong	Lee Ah Wat
Tan Ah Chow	Liang Ah Kong
Chan Ah Chow	Tan Ah Chiang
Low Ah Heng	Lim Ah Tak
Chia Jee	Koo Cheng Swee
Chan Ah Teng	Lim Ah Teem
Tan Tua	Tay Ah Hock
Lee Ah Seng	Lim Ah Leack

24. It has to be stated that many organizations proliferated in Singapore from a common territorial and, also, blood origin. In other words, there were more than just the Hokkien Association, the Teochew Association, and so on, or the Tan, Lim, and other clans. For dialect group speakers also organized on a narrower basis, for example, Hokkien speakers from the prefecture of Chang-chou had their own association, the Changchou Association, which excluded other Hokkien speakers, and Hakkas from the prefecture of Chia-ying-chou in Kwangtung also organized similarly. Moreover what was organized on the dialect group principle might in another view be considered a clan if that organization were to be confined to the particular dialect group speakers with the same surname. That was the case with the Hokkien Tan group in their early years. (In the later part of the nineteenth century, the group began to transcend dialect group differences. See the plaques in their temple in Magazine Road, Singapore. In one plaque of members in 1878, they were all Hokkiens. In the second plaque of members in 1883, the membership

included Teochews.) See also Freedman, 'Kinship', p.67.

25. See footnote 7.

26. Stronach, *Letters*, 23 August 1839; 27 August 1839; 22 October 1841.

27. See the letter of Stronach dated 14 May 1839. He wrote that he studied Hokkien because to study mandarin 'would have been to have rendered it impossible for us to do anything in the way of oral intercourse with the Chinese here, who know nothing whatever of the mandarin sounds'. See also footnote 5.

28. Here in Singapore, *kongsi* is used sometimes interchangeably with *hui-kuan* with regard to the Teochews. See *Hsin-chia-po ch'iao-chou pa I hui-kuan ssu shih chou chi nien* (*Publication of the Fortieth Anniversary Celebration of the Ch'iao-chou hui-kuan*), Singapore, 1969, p.164. Certainly the Teochews, when they first began organizing, adopted the *kongsi* name. This suggests that the term *kongsi* would be more appropriately applied to organizations of Chinese in a remote place, isolated by themselves, and involved in either commercial agriculture (as the Teochews were in the early stage) or mining as the Hakkas were in some places in Borneo, hence their organizations were called *kongsis*. See 'A Hakka Kongsi in Borneo', Barbara Ward, *Journal of Oriental Studies*, Vol. 1, July 1954, No. 2.

29. The inscription on a plaque in the earliest Chinese temple (which was begun in 1830) in Singapore in Selat Road states that the temple then performed in some way these two functions.

30. Particularly in the twentieth century.

31. Skinner, op. cit., p.167, noted that the weaker the dialect group, the more organized it was. This seems generally true of other overseas Chinese societies. See Tien, op. cit. Tien observed that it was often the weakest group economically that had the most interest in organizing either among themselves or with some more wealthy group.

32. Stronach, *Letters*, 26 November 1840.

33. For example, the official register of dangerous societies, presumably secret societies, in 1879 named about ten; Ghee Hin (Hokkien), Ghee Hin (Teochew), Ghee Hin (Hylam), Ghee Hok, Ghee Sin, Ghee Khee Kwang Hock, Hok Hin, Kong Fooy Sew, Song Peh Kwan, Haisan. *Straits Settlements Gazettes* (9 April 1880), p.228. Vaughan's list in *Manners and Customs*, p.108, further included the Kong Fooy Sew and the Song Peh Kwan, presumably the Cantonese and Hakka branches. It is useful to notice here that secret societies included Hokkiens, thus suggesting that not all Hokkiens were controlled by Malacca Chinese. For reasons why there should be dialect branches of secret societies see Chapter IV.

34. Mervyn Llewellyn Wynne, *Triad and Tabut—A Survey of the Origin and Diffusion of Chinese and Mohammedan Secret Societies in the Malay Peninsula A.D. 1800-1935* (Singapore, Government Printing Office, 1957). Among those who subscribe to this view is Maurice Freedman in 'Immigrants and Association: The Chinese in 19th Century Singapore', in *Comparative Studies in Society and History* (New York, Locust Valley, 1959).

35. See Blythe's foreword in Wynne's book. Others inclined to believe that Wynne's theory is more conjectural than factual are Purcell, op. cit., see indirect reference p.272, footnote 6, and Wong Lin Ken and C. S. Wang (see their 'Secret Societies in Malaya', review article in the *Journal of Southeast Asian History*, March 1960, Vol. 1, No. 1.

36. Blythe claims to base his view on evidence not available to Wynne.

37. *Chinese Repository*, September 1833, p.230.

38. *An Anecdotal History*, p.366; see also Pickering's annual report for 1878 (*Straits Settlements Gazette*, 21 February 1879), p.111, when he wrote that in 'cases when the headmen of a lodge offend against the general laws of the Ghee Hin society, they are tried at the Rochore Kong-Si house, before a general council of the nine branches'.

39. Munshi Abdullah, 'Concerning Tan Tae Hoey in Singapore', *Journal of the Indian Archipelago*, Vol. VI, 1852; article written in 1826, and *Singapore Chronicle*, 2 June 1831.

40. See Blythe, *The Impact*, p.16. See also 'The Chinese Secret Societies of the Tien Ti-huih', Lieutenant Newbold, *Journal of Royal Asiatic Society* (Northern Ireland and England), Vol. VI, 1861.

41. *Chinese Repository*, September 1833, p.230.

42. Pickering, *Fraser's Magazine*, p.440.

43. Vaughan, op. cit., p.108.

44. *Singapore Free Press*, 18 February 1889.

45. Jean Chesneaux (ed.), *Popular Movements and Secret Societies in China 1840-1950* (Stanford, Stanford University Press, 1972), p.6.

46. The Triad article is taken from Schlegel, *Thian Ti Hwui, the Hung League or Heaven and Earth League* (Detroit, Mich. College Park Station, 1866), p.135, and the Ghee Hok article is taken from Vaughan, op. cit., p.115.

47. *Singapore Free Press*, 28 September 1849.

48. *Singapore Free Press*, 18 February 1889.

49. Munshi Abdullah, op. cit., p.550.

50. Ibid., p.547.

51. The latter two might have some, judging from the number of clan wars fought in China in this period, but, as constituted in Singapore, it is doubtful that they had much in comparison with the secret societies. Also, the secret societies actively sought new members, unlike the clans and dialect group associations, see 'The Chinese Brotherhood', *Singapore Chronicle*, 2 June 1831.

52. See 'Agricultural Labourers' in 'General Report of the Residency of Singapore, drawn up principally with a view of illustrating its agricultural statistics', by J. Thomson, *Journal of the Indian Archipelago*, Vol. III, 1849, p.767; see also Buckley, *An Anecdotal History*, p.366.

53. Quoted in Blythe, *The Impact*, p.58.

54. *The Daily Times*, 26 November 1874.

55. Pickering, *Fraser's Magazine*, p.440.

56. For example, in the great riot of 1854, the merchants, especially Seah Eu Chin, made a great effort to help the government to calm the situation.

57. Information on Ho Yem Ko taken from *Singapore Free Press*, 12 March 1846, and on Tan Tek Hye in a letter he wrote to the *Free Press* on 25 March 1846.

58. Information on the last three are taken from Bonham's account made in 1830, but reprinted in *Singapore Free Press*, 9 March 1865.

59. See Chapter II.

60. Taken from Comber, *Chinese Secret Societies*, p.291.

61. See Chapter II.

62. Article, 'The Chinese Brotherhood' found in the *Singapore Chronicle*, 2 June 1831. However, when the government started deporting secret society members later, the societies began admitting local-born Chinese. But the government prevented the latter from doing so when it was discovered.

63. *Proceedings of Legislative Council of the Straits Settlements in 1873*; and quoted in C. S. Wang, *A Gallery of Chinese Kapitans* (Singapore, Ministry of Culture, 1963), p.32.

64. *Straits Settlements Secret Correspondence*, 3 December 1827.

65. *Chinese Repository*, Vol. VI, May 1837 to May 1838, p.154.

66. *Straits Settlements Annual Report, 1856-57*, see section on the military, p.19.

67. *Singapore Free Press*, 28 March 1839.

68. *Singapore Free Press*, 25 July 1851.

69. Munshi Abdullah, op. cit.

70. See Blythe, op. cit., p.59.

71. See *Singapore Chronicle*, 2 June 1831; 21 October 1830.

72. Jackson, *Planters and Speculators*, p.22.

73. 'Riouw en Onderhoorigheden' in *Encyclopaedia van Nederlandsche-Indie*. P. G. Vander Lith and John F. Snellman (Leiden, 1905). Translation kindly supplied by Carl Trocki.

74. While the withholding of financial rewards by the financiers was a powerful incentive to ensure worker co-operation, it was not enough. There were bound to be innumerable disputes concerning work arrangements in such a harsh agricultural environment which only some coercive organization could handle. For this, see J. Thomson, 'Agricultural Labourers', *Journal of the Indian Archipelago*.

75. *Singapore Chronicle*, 2 June 1831.

76. Buckley, *An Anecdotal History*, p.213.

IV

THE CLASH BETWEEN THE TWO SOCIETIES

THE situation was such that before the 1840s the two societies were not directly involved with the actual conduct of trade in the entrepôt economy: the gambier and pepper society not at all, and the society of the residual economy only indirectly so. This was to change when the free traders expanded their activities in Singapore and the surrounding areas. The consequence was the intrusion of free trade into the two societies. To cope with this, the original base had to be expanded from a small area on the southern waterfront of the island at the time of the British establishment of Singapore to some larger area, in fact, to the entire island. One consequence of this was the building of roads from the city to the northern end of Singapore together with the development of certain areas near this road. These developments impinged on the existing gambier and pepper plantations and resulted in the riot of 1851. The second consequence was the need for orderliness in the city so that the management of the expanded economic activities could be facilitated. Streets which were cluttered by vagabond hawkers and vendors had to be cleared and some appropriate sites allotted to these people. This was done in 1856, but a riot broke out as they considered such a measure to be a threat to their livelihood. Finally, attempts were made by the free traders to control the more lucrative aspects of business then existing in the two societies. These were the rice and the remittance businesses which were controlled by the Teochew financiers. The results of such attempts were the riots of 1854 and 1876. In all these riots, the Malacca Chinese and the Hokkiens either co-operated with the British or played an active part themselves in stopping the riots. But before these developments can be fully elaborated, it is necessary to mention two facts, both indirect consequences of free trade, by way of a background. These were the growing gap between the Teochew financiers and the pioneers and workers, and the great increase in the Chinese population from the 1840s onwards.

Though the gambier and pepper society initially was largely independent of the entrepôt society, it was, only a matter of time, before the two met, not necessarily by a deliberate policy of the free traders. It grew rather out of the logic of events. As time passed, the financiers became increasingly divorced from the actual production process, even if they had once been pioneers; no one wanted to stay on to supervise the work force in an unpleasant, tiger-infested jungle. Successful pioneers preferred to move to the town and concentrate on building financial empires, leaving others to manage the labour force. Just such a town had been created by the free traders. Thus by the 1840s, it would seem that the majority of the Teochew financiers had moved into the city: in 1843 the *Singapore Free Press* wrote of many who had greatly reduced, if not stopped altogether, their visits to the plantations for fear of tigers.[1]

This meant that the financiers gradually lost their personal authority over the workers and pioneers, and consequently their control of the secret societies. In the 1840s it was already reported that many shopkeepers had to pay extortion money to the secret societies.[2] Many of these shopkeepers would probably have been Teochew financiers. Their presence in Singapore made them a rival group there to the Malacca Chinese, though they were both financially and politically weaker. (Though the Malacca Chinese may have maintained their domination of Chinese society by assimilating successful immigrants[3]—Teochews like Seah Eu Chin and Wee Ah Hood would be examples[4]—they could not absorb the whole group, even had they wanted to.)

The Teochew financiers were fundamentally disadvantaged in their encounter with the Malacca Chinese. Some gross figures can be adduced as evidence of their financial weakness. In 1848 the combined value of gambier and pepper produced in Singapore amounted to $188,230, while the value of imports and exports for Singapore for the same year came to $12,379,801 and $11,049,969 respectively.[5] Much more money could be made from the entrepôt economy than from gambier and pepper agriculture. In the 1860s it was estimated that the total amount of Teochew investment in Johore, where most of the gambier and pepper exported through Singapore was then grown, amounted to $1 million[6] while the personal fortune of one Malacca Chinese alone, Tan Kim Seng, was estimated at the time of his death in 1864, at \$2 million.[7] Finally, in the later part of the nineteenth century, a knowledgeable observer wrote that the Hokkien merchants were far richer than the Teochew gambier and pepper merchants.[8] Ultimately, the Malacca Chinese also had the military and political backing of the British.

At the same time, the opening of the port of Hong Kong, itself a victory of the free traders in China, opened the way to mass immigration from China.[9] Many came to Singapore either to wait for distribution elsewhere or to swell the ranks of the population of the residual economy. Here are the figures up to 1871.[10]

Year	Chinese
1824	3,317
1830	6,555
1836	13,749
1840	17,704
1849	27,988
1860	50,543
1871	54,572

The most rapid increase occurred between 1840 and 1860.

The 1851 Anti-Catholic Riots

This riot, one of great intensity, involving the deaths of 500 men, has been characterized as a fight between the secret societies and the Roman Catholics. Roman Catholicism had been gaining many Chinese converts, and this, so one argument goes,[11] not only reduced the recruits for the secret societies but had the effect of creating groups on the island whose aims and interests were fundamentally adverse to the secret societies. The secret societies 'could no longer hold their meetings, or execute sentence on refractory or defaulting members with the same security which they had enjoyed when there was no check upon their proceedings. This led to a general attack upon the Christian Chinese throughout the island.'[12]

A second argument, partially related to the first, has it that in China Christian converts could seek immunity from Chinese law or from the secret societies by appealing to the Roman Catholic church which had the support of the western powers. The secret

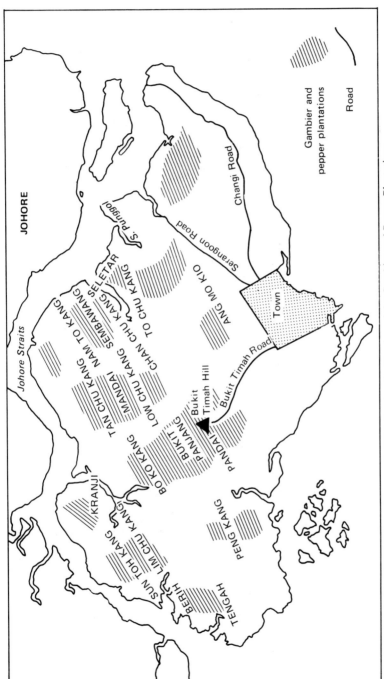

JOHORE

Johore Straits

S. Punggol

SELETAR

NAW TO KANG

TAN CHU KANG

KAMWANG

MANDAI

SEMBAWANG

TO CHU CHU KANG

LOW CHU CHU KANG

BO KO KANG

BUKIT PANJANG

PANDAI

Bukit Timah Hill

Bukit Panjang

KRANJI

SUN TOH KANG

LIM CHU KANG

BERIH

TENGAH

PENG KANG

ANG MO KIO

Serangoon Road

Changi Road

Bukit Timah Road

Town

Gambier and pepper plantations

Road

5. Singapore in 1844 showing the Roads and the Gambier and Pepper Plantations

68

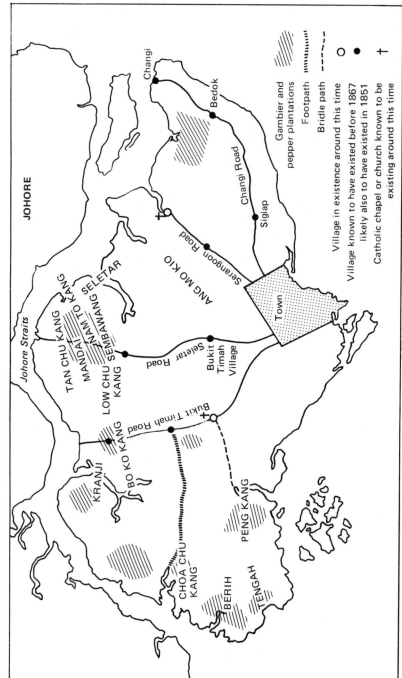

6. Singapore in 1851 showing the Extended Bukit Timah Road and the New Seletar Road.

societies in Singapore saw a parallel in local developments, and in a kind of nationalistic reaction they fell on the Catholics.[13]

The China comparison is rather problematical since its pro-pounder, Leon Comber, adduces no evidence. While the earlier argument contains some truth, it nevertheless overstressed the religious element. Why, as anti-Roman Catholic feeling had been strong before 1851, did riots not erupt then?[14] Above all, why were many of those killed prosperous 'Christian planters who had become converts',[15] and why was there a strike of non-Christian workers just before the riot? The answer must lie in the existence of socio-economic bases for the riot.

The argument here is that the 1851 riot has to be viewed within the context of the free trade society moving into the interior from the early 1840s onwards. It was around this period that gambier and pepper began developing on a large scale in the state of Johore (see maps) and to some extent in the interior of Singapore. (The Malay chief in control of Johore, the Temenggong, encouraged the growth of gambier and pepper in his state as a means of in-creasing the state revenue.) But as much of the gambier and pepper grown at this time went to the European market, it is very likely the free traders controlled the marketing process, and to facilitate this, roads were built to link Singapore town with those parts of Singapore island in the north which were near Johore. This develop-ment encouraged the creation of small settlements along these roads, especially near junctions and near the coast. Both the roads and the settlements intruded on the plantations of the pioneers and workers and forced them out. Because the British allowed Catholics, many probably Hakkas, to build some of these settlements,[16] the resentment of the Teochew pioneers and workers, as expressed in their secret societies, was directed against the Catholics.[17] This resentment erupted in the riot of 1851, because at that time prices of gambier and pepper were at their lowest.

Two maps show the nature of the developments. Map 1 shows Singapore island in 1844.[18] It shows basically two things: the places where gambier and pepper were under cultivation; and three roads, Bukit Timah, Serangoon and Changi.

Map 2 shows Singapore in 1851. We see a new road, Seletar Road, and the extension of the Bukit Timah Road to the Johore Straits; and also the places where settlements were created.

It can be established with some degree of certainty that in two settlements, one on Bukit Timah Hill at a junction of Bukit Timah

Road with a bridle path, and the other where Serangoon Road met a creek, there were substantial numbers of Catholics. The settlement on Bukit Timah Hill merited the building in 1846 of a Roman Catholic church solely for Chinese converts. They were chiefly engaged in planting, according to Song, at a spot,[19] be it noted, 'liberally granted to them by the local authorities, from whom they have always experienced kindness, particularly from his Honour the Governor'.[20] As for the Serangoon Settlement, we already know that in 1853 a Father Maistre formed a Chinese parish,[21] indicating the prior presence of substantial numbers of Catholics. It is likely that land for this church was also 'liberally granted' by the authorities. There is no record of who settled in the other villages, though it would not be surprising if many were Catholics.[22] One should note that both settlements, and indeed many others, were on land where gambier and pepper were cultivated (see Map 1).

The building of the roads was part of, if not the culmination of, the process of eviction of the Teochew agriculturists from their plantations, which started with the Straits Land Act of 1839. This Act, apart from permitting longer leases on land, also allowed the government to declare all occupied lands not held under grant as subject to assessment, and to evict people from land to which they had no legal claims.

This law had been enacted because the free traders saw the interior of Singapore and also Johore as areas for the cultivation of commercial crops for the British market which had lowered its tariffs in the 1830s. Hitherto, the free traders had left the interior undisturbed and Europeans owned land only in the city. The previous land laws had permitted very short leases, something unsuitable for the European type of plantation agriculture with large investments and slow returns.

The 1839 Act was disastrous for the agriculturists in the independent settlements for it meant the invasion of their plantations, the ownership of which hitherto had been adjudicated by their own social mechanisms. Unable to resist physically the powerful British, some seem to have tried to acquire legal title to their land. Thus it was reported in 1841 that not a week passed without someone going to the newly appointed government surveyor, J. Thomson, for some adjudication of the legitimacy of his claim.[23] Such adjudication, or any compensation for lands appropriated, was unlikely to be satisfactory.[24]

The Teochews who suffered from this were probably mainly pioneers.[25] Needless to say, they would react. But that they did not do so with great violence till 1851 must be because the expropriation process had not fully developed, and the opening of gambier and pepper plantations in Johore in the 1840s served to some extent as an outlet for dispossessed pioneers and workers.[26]

But things changed in the late 1840s. There was a drastic decline in the prices of gambier and pepper from 1831 to 1861 as shown by the following figures.

TABLE IV
SAMPLE PRICES QUOTED LOCALLY FOR
GAMBIER AND BLACK PEPPER
(1831-1861)

Year	Gambier	Black Pepper
January 1831	1.30 to 1.75	5.00 to 5.25
„ 1834	4.00 to 5.00	6.00 to 6.25
„ 1837	3.00 to 3.25	6.75 to 7.00
„ 1840	2.70 to 2.80	5.65 to 6.00
„ 1844	1.50	4.20 to 4.30
„ 1849	0.90 to 1.00	3.60
„ 1855	3.15 to 3.20	6.50 to 6.75
„ 1859	2.67 to 2.70	7.70
„ 1861	2.85	6.75

The figures show that during the period around 1849 prices were the lowest ever. Even when prices were good, the pioneers could hardly make ends meet. Now many of them would be in deep trouble, and even more of the workers, for their wages were adjusted to the prices. A *Free Press* article in 1848 captures the feeling at the time very well:[28]

The prospects of the Chinese engaged in agricultural labours in this settlement are still of the most disheartening nature, the price of gambier continuing to be utterly unremunerative; in fact it must leave a serious loss to some parties, unless indeed the wages of the unfortunate coolies have been reduced in proportion to the fall in prices, as we believe this has been the case. The cultivation of gambier has in a great many instances been abandoned and in some places the pepper vines have been increased but a considerable time must of course elapse before these are productive. The coolies, therefore, are in a very miserable condition, having an inadequate supply of food and no possible honest means of providing more.

This meant two things: a similar depression in Johore and its consequent inability to act as an outlet, and a much impoverished group of workers. All this made for an extremely explosive situation. The spark came with the extension and the building of the roads, as the accounts of the riots indicate clearly. 'Everywhere,' wrote the papers, 'at Serangoon, Bukit Timah, Bookoh Khan, Lauw Choo-Khan, Nam To Kang, Chan Chwee Kang, even Kranji, Propo and Benoi, the bangsalls [a kind of plantation] and plantations of the Christians have been attacked by sets of 20 to 50 men, who rob all the property and destroy what they cannot carry away.'[29] If these places are checked on the maps, everyone of them is in or around the villages which sprang up as a result of the roads, where the Catholics, many of them planters, lived. Hence the riot can now be explained in terms of dispossessed pioneers and impoverished workers reacting to the intrusion of the free traders by attacking that aspect of the intrusion most manifest to them, the Catholics who now occupied their land. That the secret societies were used is hardly surprising, for by then the pioneers had gained control of them. The Teochew financiers indeed were against the riot, as indicated by the governor's praise of 'the heathen proprietors of gambier plantations who are respectable people and located in the town [and they] have come forward on the present occasion and subscribed a sum of money to remunerate the Christian Chinese for the losses they have sustained'.[30]

The 1854 Riot and the 1876 Post Office Riots

While the Teochew financiers were well ensconced in the city in the latter half of the nineteenth century, this in no way weakened or destroyed their control of the rice business from Siam and the remittances of money to China by the coolies and others. As mentioned in Chapter II, the operations were more a function of control of shipping and of contacts in Siam and China than of the labour force. Coolies had to buy rice anyway; and they were the keenest of all to remit their earnings to impoverished relatives in China and were only too glad that such a postal service was provided.[31]

Lacking control of shipping and of contacts in Siam and China in the 1840s, the free traders did not immediately attempt to wrest control from the Teochew financiers. But two events changed all this; the British invasion of the Chinese monopolies in Siam, legalized by the Bowring Treaty of 1855, and British consolidation of the coolie traffic by the 1870s.

THE 1854 RIOT

To understand this riot, some background on the rice business is important. From the documentation available, it would seem that Singapore obtained its rice from two major sources, Siam and Java.[32] At the same time Seah Eu Chin's list of Chinese occupations in 1848 shows two dialect groups, the Teochews and the Hokkiens, as providing the main dealers in rice. He lists about 1,900 Teochews and 1,400 Hokkiens. It is not known from what source the Hokkiens obtained their rice—it was probably Java,[33] but, from what we have previously seen, it is most likely that the Teochews obtained their rice from Siam.

If the grip of the Teochews on the Siamese trade could be broken, the free traders could then control the rice market and use the Malacca Chinese as their distributors. What was required was control of supplies and transport. Beginning in 1852,[34] the British made inroads into the Chinese monopolies which included rice.

At the same time, the British displaced Chinese junk traffic from Siam to Singapore. Consider these figures for square-rigged vessels and junks arriving in Singapore from Siam.[35]

TABLE V

SQUARE-RIGGED VESSELS AND JUNKS ARRIVING IN
SINGAPORE FROM SIAM

Square-Rigged Vessels			Siamese Junks (mainly Chinese operated)	
Year	No.	Tonnage	No.	Tonnage
1829-30	30	3,589	31	3,953
1832-3	4	628	37	4,397
1835-6	9	3,050	23	4,004
1838-9	22	6,301	23	5,219
1841-2	15	5,313	28	7,057
1844-5	13	4,802	22	3,258
1847-8	21	7,521	20	4,820
1850-1	16	4,853	63	5,864
1853-4	37	8,938	85	9,213
1856-7	145	37,503	28	2,994
1862-3	119	31,119	4	1,105
1865-6	51	15,361	1	35

Around the middle of the 1850s there is an astonishing rise in the number and tonnage of square-rigged vessels (many British-owned) from Siam to Singapore, while Siamese junks, many operated by Chinese,[36] decreased dramatically in number. The Bowring Treaty of 1855 must have been responsible for this dramatic increase. But the Treaty, which ended many Chinese monopolies in Thailand and opened them to free trade, was only the culmination of inroads made from 1852. Hence the increase in the square-rigged tonnage to Singapore from Siam must be seen as part of a trend that began around 1852. This explosive situation would have been accentuated by the big fall in the export of rice from Java around 1850[37] while the number of consumers in Singapore also rose very considerably (see population figures cited earlier). Rice was thus scarcer and more expensive than hitherto. With all this in mind, we may turn to the accounts of the 1854 riot.

One group of observers saw it primarily as a conflict between rival secret societies.[38] According to Comber, some defeated rebels of the Small Dagger Society in China had fled to Singapore and swelled the ranks of the Ghee Hok (Hokkien) secret society. The Ghee Hin (Teochew and others), which had previously been numerically superior, resented this, and a battle resulted.[39] Buckley wrote that the real reason for the riot was the refusal of the Hokkiens to join with the Teochews and others in a subscription to assist rebels driven from Amoy by the Imperial China Troops.[40] Both agreed however that the incident which sparked the riot was the feeling of a non-Hokkien that he had been cheated by a Hokkien over the sale of a certain quantity of rice. There also is some agreement (the exception is Comber) that the groups engaged were not so much secret societies, though they were involved, but Hokkiens against Teochews who had the support of the other dialect groups. Thus Vaughan wrote that 'the solemn obligations of the secret societies were cast to the winds, and members of the same hoey [secret societies] fought to the death against their brethren'.[41] The *Straits Guardian* said it was the Hokkiens against the Teochews and others.[42]

Thus the lines seem clearly drawn. But are these explanations enough? We can be sure that no battle lasting over ten days, with about 400 men killed, can be over something so trivial as a quantity of rice. Comber's reasons seem unclear and unsatisfactory. Did he mean that a power conflict was brought about by a numerical increase in the ranks of the Ghee Hok? He did not say. Buckley's reasons also do not go deep enough. Disagreement over an 'issue' would not lead to such intense rioting unless some underlying antagonism was involved, for which both the rice and the sub-scription issue provided the sparks. That the antagonism must have been over something truly vital like the rice market is indicated by the fact that the Hokkiens captured the supplies of rice during the fighting, according to a most detailed field-investigation published in the *Straits Guardian*.[43] This would fit with what has been said about the rice trade during this period.

That the Malacca Chinese would mobilize the Hokkiens would be hardly surprising as the Hokkiens stood to gain from the Malacca Chinese controlling the rice. The Hokkiens would become the distributors. Probably the presence of some rebels from the Small Dagger Society contributed to the violence on the Hokkien side.[44] It is also likely that the rice shortage would induce the Teochew agriculturists, already aggrieved by British rule, to join forces with the Teochew financiers. This too is indicated by the *Straits Times*, which noted that the countryside began to wear an 'ap-pearance of the utmost disquietude'. The places which 'witnessed the most diabolical acts of cruelty', according to the *Straits Guar-dian*,[45] were Tanglin, Bukit Timah and Paya Lebar which, from a glance at Map 2, were in areas generally encompassed by the roads built after 1844, places where the aggrieved agriculturists were located. The other dialect groups probably went along because they feared that rice in the hands of the Hokkiens might mean higher prices. That the rioters were aware that the British had something to do with the crisis is shown by a British observation that many Europeans were pelted in the riots.[46]

THE 1876 POST OFFICE RIOT

From the beginning British shipping far overshadowed the Chinese shipping from China direct to Singapore. This is easily seen by the total tonnages (to and from China) of square-rigged vessels and Chinese junks from the years 1829-66.[47]

The main problem for the free traders in the postal service business was not so much control of shipping as developing the contacts in China who could deliver the money to the appropriate persons inland. This took some time. It was not until the 1840s that the free traders had a foothold in Hong Kong, and not until 1858, when the port of Swatow was opened to the Westerners,

TABLE VI
TOTAL TONNAGES OF SQUARE-RIGGED VESSELS AND JUNKS
FROM CHINA TO SINGAPORE AND VICE VERSA

Year	Square-rigged Vessels	Chinese Junks
1829–30	67,522	4,835
1832–3	62,946	3,922
1835–6	106,605	5,315
1838–9	18,967	14,588
1841–2	130,396	30,545
1844–5	158,377	23,457
1847–8	133,775	25,598
1850–1	163,916	22,308
1853–4	149,844	31,555
1856–7	270,827	17,537
1862–3	186,866	21,495
1865–6	440,156	4,584

that they moved in on the prefecture of Chao-chou, the home of
the Teochews. Their primary concern at that time was still to
cash in on and develop the coolie traffic. Neither would be easy
if the British attempted to seize control of the remittance traffic;
the Teochew financiers would certainly pass the word that the
British were either destroying the traffic or were increasing the
charges. It was not until the British felt securely in control of the
coolie traffic that they struck. Thus, Tan Seng Poh, testifying
before the Government Commission on Labour in 1876, could
say that the coolie business 'in Swatow is almost entirely carried
on by Europeans', and the Chinese, 'work through European
firms' such as Bradley and Co., Pustau and Co.'.[48]

In 1876, then, the British gave the right to open a post office
to a *baba* (a Straits-born or Malacca Chinese) and attempted to
channel postal traffic through it. In reaction to this, the Teochew
financiers mobilized the Chinese masses, representing to them
the threat this posed to their relatives in China. One of the many
placards which appeared at the time of the 1876 riot stated:

We hear that lately one or two rascals with covetous desires and dis-
regarding justice, have been with the ruler of Singapore (i.e., the British),
and with fair speeches and intriguing plans have established a post office,
intending to begin gently and to go to great depth; they mean to oppress
the Chinese in their private gains. To the rich this does not matter, but

truly it is cheating poor people. We have come to these barbarous tribes (the British), is it not because our families are poor and can scarcely pass the day for want of food. Is it not to feed our wives and children we have left our relatives and come here to labour and carry, or to trade a little for profits which are sent to them to assist their urgent necessities.[49]

This had a powerful effect, and many Chinese reacted by going out on strike.

Our analysis is supported by a *Daily Times* report

... that the instigators were the Chinese Towkays (financiers) whose business would be affected by the establishment of a Government Post Office and Money Order Office ... and deliberately misrepresented them to the coolies and their more ignorant countrymen who were to be benefited ... and that in their action they had the sympathy, more or less active and passive, of all the Chinese shopkeepers and small traders of the place.[50]

Another interesting placard was put up by these financiers, which indicated that some rich Teochews sided with the other side. Part of it stated:

But who could know that Tan Seng Poh, Tay Lee Soon, Khaw Chong Nghee, Low How Kim, Tan Noh Keah, Goh Low and Kang Ah Peah and the like were the men who united in this affair to ruin men and take their lives. A crime which rises up to Heaven! Must it not be that their families will utterly perish?

Now Seng Poh is not one of our Chinese race but is the offspring of a mixture of Barbarian and Chinese blood so he can deceive and change and raise trouble.

Now Kim, Lee Soon and Noh Keah, in their youth acquired a reputation, and thus they were luckily enabled to obtain the flourishing and wealthy business of the shop 'Lung Chiang', the profit of not walking in the path of righteousness. They have moreover ruined trades, and taken away life, truly their guilt will not easily be wiped away.[51]

Of the names mentioned here, information could be found for only three. Tan Seng Poh and Low How Kim were Teochews who were assimilated to the Malacca Chinese, while Tan Noh Keah was a Roman Catholic padre, probably a Teochew.[52] It is likely the rest were Teochews, for judging from the tone of the placard, the Teochew financiers must have felt betrayed by those defecting to the other side, probably after having taken advantage of their fellow dialect group members.

The Secret Society Organized General Strike of 1857

In 1857, the government in Singapore promulgated certain Police and Municipal Acts which were designed to move Chinese hawkers and vendors off the streets of the town. In reaction to what they saw as a threat to their livelihood, the population of the residual economy went on a general strike.[53] On 2 January 1857, shops in every part of the town, according to the *Free Press*, were closed and the hack-syces, boatmen, and coolies, refused to work. Those who did come soon left because they were threatened, while the markets were deserted early in the morning and business of every kind was at an end. The strike was apparently an impressive effort, for a writer described the heart of Singapore, hitherto flourishing, as presenting 'a strange sight'.[54]

There is little disagreement as to who the organizers of the strike were. The *Free Press* reported a public meeting of Europeans and Chinese as stating that 'the evident reliance of the people during the disturbances on the orders of certain headmen is another proof of the dangerous combination of the Chinese secret societies, whose growing power has long been subversive of public order and security'.[55] A similar opinion was expressed by the Governor who, in a dispatch to India about the strike, stated that the secret societies constituted the organizational framework of the Chinese.[56]

Many writers suggest that the cause of the strike was that the population of the residual economy misunderstood the intentions of the government.[57] The government, they continued, had no intention of depriving the hawkers and vendors of their livelihood, but only to maintain an orderly and efficient town. After all, the government offered an alternative site in the form of three buildings where, with the proper rents, the hawkers and vendors could do business. One of these writers,[58] adds also that the then British blockade of Canton in China (part of the Lorcha *Arrow* War) contributed to a feeling of ill-will on the part of the Chinese in Singapore against the British.

However, the misunderstanding is not a sufficient explanation, for many other Chinese such as boatmen, hack-syces, and others, whose livelihood was not threatened by the regulations, also went on strike. Moreover, the British action in China could only have fuelled Chinese resentment, not caused it. The explanation must rather first be sought within the context of free trade. This can be seen in two ways. First, free trade itself had led to a vast increase in the population of the residual economy around the 1840s and 1850s. By their destruction of many gambier and pepper plantations, the free traders had created many unemployed Chinese, many of whom were bound to drift into the town. Moreover, emigration from China had greatly increased from the 1840s onwards. Many of these migrants found their way to Singapore, which acted as a distribution centre for labour in the rest of South-East Asia. This migration, however, was not directly a function of the employment situation (it suited the free traders to keep up this stream, even if employment were bad, as wages could be kept low by a large labour supply), which in fact was difficult in the 1840s and 1850s. It is estimated that only one-twentieth of the arriving migrants found immediate employment.[59] This 'surplus' population had to find some means to live, and being unskilled and without influence, they attempted to eke out a living by hawking and vending, or searching for seasonal employment. They naturally cluttered up the streets and sidewalks. Thus, the *Straits Settlements Annual Report of 1855-56* complained of streets being 'encumbered by the petty vendors of provisions'.

But there was a second aspect of free trade, the efficient functioning of the town. That depended on some orderliness: roads should not obstruct the movement of goods, let alone actual human movement. Hence it is not surprising that the government attempted to move these vendors into government buildings.

But an action which may seem to the British to be necessary for efficiency may seem to the secret society leaders to threaten their control of the population of the residual economy. One reason for the secret society control of this population of the residual economy, as mentioned previously, was their social and political value. They were involved in mutual aid activities and were able to organize the Chinese to resist any governmental action against them which might appear unjust. Here the Municipal and Police Acts were seen by those whose livelihood was threatened as clearly unjust since many could not afford to pay the rents demanded. These hawkers and vendors constituted a sizeable part of the population. Hence the secret society leaders, in order to maintain their credibility, had to organize the Chinese to help this group to resist. It is likely also that the secret societies realized that any form of governmental interference in regulating the population of the residual economy could lessen their control, because the government represented an alternative power centre.[60]

At this juncture it would be useful by way of conclusion to say something about the nature of the secret societies. We have seen that in the disturbances of 1851 and 1857 they organized the Chinese to resist the government. Yet in other governmental actions, such as permitting the sale of opium and the conduct of the coolie traffic (actions, which by most standards, cannot be said to be advancing the welfare of the population of the residual economy) the secret societies did not organize the Chinese to resist. Why?

One probable answer is that the secret societies lacked an ideology to link all these governmental actions as arising from a pioneer economy. While the secret societies arose from an unsettled population which the pioneer economy in Singapore attracted, there was not necessarily a direct causal connexion between them and the pioneer economy. Hence they would lack the ability to perceive that the injustices of the pioneer economy could manifest themselves in different ways.

Therefore, it is likely that the secret societies acted only when there was pressure from some aggrieved segment of the population.

But it is also possible that at times when there was no great pressure, the very methods used to resist the British could be used to intimidate the population of the residual economy, particularly if the secret societies were to be captured by ambitious men who could not succeed in either trade or gambier and pepper agriculture. They could then use the secret societies for their own gain. Thus this is one way to explain the many criminal activities of the secret societies in the nineteenth century, activities involving prostitution, gambling, and the kidnapping of coolies.

Finally, the British on their part were not unmindful of the social instability and criminality which plagued the Chinese population from the 1840s onwards. Numerous documents of a private and governmental nature attest to this.[61] But it is doubtful if they understood the reasons for it. They took steps such as calling in the military, and using legal measures such as jailing, flogging, deportation, and registering the secret societies, etc. to maintain some semblance of stability, but these steps were at best stop-gap measures.[62] The policy of free trade called for only minimal involvement in Chinese society, and important steps like the abolition of the secret societies and establishing some kind of bureaucracy to regulate the Chinese constituted more than minimal involvement. Moreover, there were other causes of instability such as the uneasy position of the Teochew financiers and the gap between the mercantile structure and the structure of the residual economy for which free trade was responsible. Things only changed fundamentally when the British abandoned their free trade policy for political intervention in the Malay Peninsula. As will be seen in the next chapter, it was this that restored stability to the Chinese population.

1. *Singapore Free Press*, 3 August 1843.
2. A public resolution passed on 10 February 1843 stated that it 'is an understood fact that many of the Chinese shopkeepers and traders in the town, particularly the native-born subjects of China, pay regular sums to the Hueys or Brotherhoods (organized associations of Chinese often for unlawful purposes) as protection money for their own property, or as a contribution in the nature of blackmail, and that it rarely or never happens that the Chinese themselves suffer from the depredations complained of.' Song, *One Hundred Years*, p.57.
3. M. Freedman, 'Immigrants and Associations', p.27.
4. Song, op. cit., pp.21 and 102.
5. Buckley, *An Anecdotal History*, pp.501-2.
6. C. M. Turnbull, 'The Johore Gambier and Pepper Trade in the Mid-Nineteenth Century', *Journal of the South Seas Society*, Vol. XV, Part 1, 1959, p.46. See also *Straits Settlements Correspondence*, 273/15, 3 October 1864.
7. John Cameron, *Our Tropical Possessions*, footnote on p.233.
8. Li, *A Description of Singapore*.
9. See Wang, *A Short History*, p.23. In one year alone (1845) as many as 12,000 emigrants arrived from China. See figures found in Comber, *Secret Societies*, p.68.
10. Taken from Saw, *Population*, p.57.
11. Found in varying ways in the *Straits Times*, 4 March 1851; Buckley, op. cit., p.543; Song, op. cit., pp.83 and 161.
12. Buckley, op. cit., p.543.
13. Comber, op. cit., p.77.
14. See *Singapore Free Press*, 27 July 1849.
15. McNair, *Prisoners*, p.68.
16. Vaughan, *Manners*, p.15, wrote that most of the plantations cleared were occupied by Teochews and Hakkas, and on p.33 he wrote that several years before 'Roman Catholic missionaries were exceedingly successful in converting the Chinese, especially the Kehs (Hakkas) to Christianity. A great many chapels were built in the country districts of all the settlements and the Hong Kahs, as Chinese Christians are called, became a powerful body. Just as in joining a secret society the converts regarded themselves as a community of brothers, and were as ready to fight as the worst of the heathen around them.' Vaughan must not have been very impressed with the quality of these Christians for he continued that, 'of late years, however, whether the zeal of the Missionary has waxed colder, or the Chinese have discovered that they acquire no peculiar privileges by becoming Christians the gospel has not spread amongst them with the rapidity of former days; many converts have recanted and returned to their former idolatry and heathenism'.
17. Land granted to Catholics by the government had always been on very favourable terms, and hence, bound to increase the resentment of the dispossessed

planters and workers. See later, and also, Agnes Fung Li-Ning, *Growth of Settlements in Rural Singapore, 1819-1857* (Singapore, University of Singapore, 1961/2), p.28.

18. The two maps (Map 1 and Map 2) have been pieced together from the following maps:

(a) J. Thomson's Map of Singapore showing the rural settlements (taken from Agnes Fung, *Growth of Settlements*, p.22).

(b) Map of Singapore Island in 1846 (found in Donald Moore, *The First 150 Years of Singapore* (Singapore, Donald Moore, 1969), p.208).

(c) Map of Singapore Island in 1851 by J. R. Logan (found in *Journal of the Indian Archipelago*, Vol. VI, 1852, facing p.178).

(d) Map of Singapore Island, 1868 (found in Turnbull, *The Straits Settlements, 1824-1867*, at the back of the book).

(e) Map of part of Singapore 'Kangkars and Bangsals in Singapore, 1885' found in Jackson, *Planters* (figure 4). The information on the places where gambier and pepper plantations existed were taken from the statistics published on 18 May 1841 and 17 May 1855 editions of the *Singapore Free Press*.

The information on the roads, apart from those on the map, was extracted from the journal kept by Major Low in 1840 and 1841. Particularly relevant is this, the two chief roads [in Singapore] are those leading to Bukit Timah, the highest hill on the island, and Serangoon, which is the name of a creek and also of a district. Each of them is about 7 miles long and without any material deviations from the right line. (Quoted in Buckley, p.363).

For the Catholic churches, see Buckley, op. cit., p.251 and from W. Makepeace, Gilbert E. Brooke, and Roland St. J. Braddell (eds.), *One Hundred Years of Singapore, being some account of the Capital of the Straits Settlements from its foundation by Sir Stamford Raffles on the 6th February 1819 to the 6th February 1919* (London, J. Murray), Vol. 2, 1921. See in this book, 'Religious Singapore', by the Reverend W. Murray, who wrote that the Chinese parish of Serangoon was founded in 1853 by Father Maistre in a place seven miles from Singapore (p.350).

19. Song, op. cit., p.33.

20. Buckley, op. cit., p.251.

21. See footnote 18. Most Catholic priests were either French or Portuguese.

22. See footnote 16.

23. Buckley, op. cit., p.352; see also McNair, op. cit., p.353.

24. A letter by a secret society member, 25 March 1846 of the *Singapore Free Press*, stated that in 1845, the Chinese were forced to buy cultivated land at two or three times the real value or were forced to vacate. Another instance occurred in 1828 when a road built by the government went through some gambier and pepper plantations. The Chinese wanted one rupee per vine but the Superintendent of Lands thought half a rupee would be liberal, *Straits Settlements Records*, 'Superintendent of Lands to Murchison', 1 April 1828.

25. The Teochew financiers were by now well ensconced in the city and hence were more aware of British law. The British also probably had no wish to offend this group for they needed some of them, especially those assimilated to the Malacca Chinese, to help develop new gambier and pepper plantations and other crops. Seah Eu Chin is an example of a Teochew assimilated by the Malacca Chinese. See Song, op. cit., p.20, and *Straits Chinese Magazine*, Vol. 3, No. 11, 1899, p.80.

26. Around the 1840s, gambier and pepper plantations developed in Johore. It is likely they would draw some of their labour from Singapore.

27. Taken from Jackson, *Planters*, p.13.

28. *Singapore Free Press*, 6 October 1848.

29. Buckley, op. cit., p.543.

30. Quoted in Blythe, *The Impact*, p.71.

31. See *Journal of the Indian Archipelago*, Vol. 1, 1847, p.35, on remittances to China. The control of the financiers must have been enhanced by their presence in the city and their proximity to the port.

32. See T. J. Newbold and relevant issues of *Singapore Chronicle* regarding the places from which rice came to Singapore. Newbold, *British Settlements in the Straits of Malacca*, Vol. 1 (London, John Murray, 1839), p.304, listed the three most important in this order, Java, Siam, and Bali. As will be seen later in Chapter VI, the British were not successful in breaking Teochew control of the rice trade. In 1889, Li, *A Description of Singapore*, the author wrote that Singapore obtained rice from Siam, Annam, and Burma.

33. See *Singapore Chronicle*, 28 April 1831 concerning junks from Amoy having goods mainly for the Bugis market while those from Teochew ports and Canton had goods mainly for Chinese settlers. This suggests that of the Teochews and the Hokkiens, it is most likely the Hokkiens had the most contacts with Java for the rice.

34. See Skinner, *Chinese Society*, p.101.

35. See Wong, 'The Trade of Singapore'.

36. See Bowring, *The Kingdom and People of Siam*; G. W. Skinner, *Chinese Society*, p.41; T'ien Ju-kang, *17-19 shih-chi chung-kuo fan-chuan tsai tung-nan-ya chou (Seventeenth to Nineteenth Century Chinese Junk Trade in South-East Asia)*, Shanghai, 1957.

37. J. S. Furnivall, *Netherlands India* (Cambridge, Cambridge University Press, 1967), p.138.

38. Buckley, op. cit., p.585; and Comber, op. cit., p.82. Both, however, did mention that dialect group differences were to some extent involved. See also Read, *Play and Politics*, p.92.

39. Comber, op. cit., p.82.

40. Buckley, op. cit., p.585.

41. Vaughan, op. cit., p.95.

42. *Straits Guardian*, 13 May 1854.

43. *Straits Guardian*, 13 May 1854.

44. Some of the members of this society, driven out from China in a rebellion, fled to Singapore.

45. *Straits Guardian*, 13 May 1854.

46. Read, op. cit., p.95.

47. Taken from Wong, op. cit., p.276.

48. 'The Report of Committee', Colonial Office 275/19.

49. *Singapore Daily Times*, 18 December 1876.

50. *Singapore Daily Times*, 29 January 1877.

51. *Singapore Daily Times*, 19 December 1877.

52. See 'The Report of Committee', Colonial Office 275/19 and Song, op. cit., pp.33 and 191.

53. Comber, op. cit., p.96.

54. Ibid.

55. *Singapore Free Press*, 8 January 1857.

56. Blythe, op. cit., p.89.

57. Comber, op. cit., p.96, and Blythe, op. cit., p.89.

58. Blythe, op. cit., p.89.

59. Eunice Thio, 'The Singapore Chinese Protectorate: Events and Conditions Leading to its Establishment', *Journal of the South Seas Society*, No. 16, 1960, p.61.

60. Perhaps some reflections on why the unrest in Singapore did not take on a millennarian form might be appropriate. (Philip Kuhn in *Rebellion and its Enemies in Late Imperial China; Militarization and Social Structure 1796-1864* (Boston,

Harvard, 1970)) saw the secret societies as intermediate between the organizations of social bandits and that of the millennarians. So did Eric Hobsbawm, *Primitive Rebels; Studies in Archaic Forms of Social Movement in the 19th and 20th Centuries* (Manchester, University Press, 1959). Eugene Genovese in a lecture on slavery in America in January 1972 in the University of London argued that millennarism did not develop among the blacks in America for two reasons, the pervasiveness of the white power structure and the unsophisticated nature of black culture. This lack of sophistication did not lead to the development of the discipline necessary for mobilizing adherents to a millennarian movement. The first reason does not apply to the Chinese in Singapore since British power, though present, was not very pervasive before 1877. Hence the second reason could be more appropriately considered. But the Chinese did not lack cultural sophistication, for around this time there were the Taiping millennarians in China, and the Chinese in Singapore could easily follow them. That they did not must be due to the conditions of the Chinese coolies. They were people who were involved in wage labour right from the start in Singapore. By their everyday struggle for existence, they could probably see clearly that the problems lay with the oppressive economic system for which redress could not be sought from following a Messiah. Moreover, these coolies must have been hardbitten fellows even before they came to Singapore, for it is suggested by Skinner that many of the immigrants to South-East Asia from China were drawn not directly from the villages but from those who had already drifted to the cities. In addition, the barbaric manner in which many came, they were, for example, huddled like pigs in the boat, did not help. They were unlike Chinese peasants who had just been uprooted and who had no experience of the insecurity involved in living outside the village system and which is quite pervasive among urban dwellers. Never having experienced insecurity before, these just-uprooted peasants could easily be attracted to a Messiah who, by his vision of a heavenly kingdom, could promise security. This would not sell to our coolies in Singapore.

61. See *Singapore Free Press*, 9 March 1865 and 26 February 1848.

62. At one stage, the British resorted to conscripting secret society leaders as constables when there was trouble.

V

BRITISH INTERVENTION IN
THE MALAY PENINSULA
AND SINGAPORE

FROM the 1870s onwards, the British abandoned the policy of free trade in the Malay Peninsula and decided to annex it politically. They did so by means of an adviser system.[1] (The first adviser was imposed on the Sultan of Perak in 1874 and the last on the Sultan of Johore in 1914.) Much controversy surrounds the origins of this intervention; some scholars writing in the Leninist-Hobson tradition see it as arising from the metropolitan countries' need for investment outlets and the consequent need for colonies to guarantee this investment;[2] those like Parkinson and Cowan argue that unstable conditions in the peninsula forced Britain to intervene for fear another power might do so;[3] a third school emphasizes the importance of the role of the British and Chinese merchants in the Straits Settlements in persuading London to intervene.[4]

Whatever the merits of these various interpretations, intervention had profound consequences for the stability of Chinese society in Singapore. Some discussion of its significance is therefore necessary.

Of late, an argument has been advanced that British intervention was not a turning point, but a milestone in the economic development of Malaya. A Malaysian historian, Khoo Kay Kim,[5] was able to show the presence of Chinese economic activities in the peninsula before the 1870s. By detaching the Chinese presence from the European, he argued that intervention in the 1870s helped to further Chinese economic activities, but did not essentially start them. Hence, British intervention was more important for its attempt to restore political order that economic intrusion before the 1870s had unsettled the Malay political system than for initiating economic change as such.

This argument, in the strictest sense, is correct.[6] But if taken too literally it can obscure the significance of the intervention. While

it did not initiate modern economic activities, intervention nevertheless brought about political protection, without which the huge
modern economic development of the Malay Peninsula would not
have been possible. We refer to the enormous Sino-British investment, from the beginning of the twentieth century, of capital
and skill in the development of vast rubber plantations and tin mines,
and a good infrastructure of roads, railways, and administration.
Intervention also caused a vast migration of Chinese to seize the
economic opportunities in the newly-opened peninsula, an increase
which, as is well known, altered the Malayan scene profoundly.
Some figures on Chinese migration to Singapore (a base for the
Malay Peninsula) in the first four years of the 1850s, 1870s, 1880s,
1890s and 1900s attest to this:[7]

TABLE VII
CHINESE MIGRANTS TO SINGAPORE BETWEEN THE
1850s AND THE 1900s

Years of the . . .	Total Chinese Migrants to Singapore
1850s (1851, '52, '53, '54)	40,302
1870s (1871, '72, '73, '74)	76,657
1880s (1881, '82, '83, '84)	233,357
1890s (1891, '92, '93, '94)	424,970
1900s (1901, '02, '03, '04)	653,077

Notice the tremendous difference between the 1870s and 1880s.

The argument here is that the political and economic results of
intervention led to developments which ended much of the instability in Singapore caused by free trade.

First, the political linkage between Singapore and the Malay
Peninsula was greatly strengthened because the British made Singapore the political centre of their power. Singapore could only
fulfil this role if there were some measure of stability in the Chinese
population, now constituting almost three-quarters of the total
inhabitants.[8] The British thus abandoned the previous policy of
minimal involvement for one of regulation. The first step was
the creation of a Chinese Protectorate in 1877[9] which developed a
small bureaucracy designed to limit the criminal activities of the
secret societies by the regulation of prostitution and ending the
kidnapping of coolies. Nonetheless the basic problem of controlling

the Chinese population remained: this meant a decision on how to deal with the secret societies. What were the alternatives? The question was considered in official circles and unofficially through the newspapers. For a fuller appreciation of the debate, two constraining factors must be mentioned.

The first was the role Singapore played as the most important centre for the distribution of Chinese immigrants in South-East Asia. Singapore was, in the words of one, 'the hub of the wheel [for these immigrants] and from this convenient centre spokes went out to all the other countries of the west Nanyang, part to the Malay Peninsula and Java'.[10] This, we know, was true before the 1870s but was much more so afterwards when the Malay Peninsula in particular developed an enormous demand for Chinese labour. Such a free flow could not be basically interfered with, except in dire economic circumstances, such as the Great Depression in the 1930s.

The second was the composition of the Chinese population in Singapore. They formed the majority group in Singapore. They were divided into many dialect groups, unlike Hong Kong, which was dominated by Cantonese. Some idea of this mixture can be gleaned from the census figures for the first thirty years or so after the 1870s.[11]

TABLE VIII

NUMBER OF CHINESE FROM DIFFERENT DIALECT GROUPS,
1881, 1891 AND 1901

	1881	1891	1901
Hokkiens	24,981	45,856	59,117
Cantonese	14,853	23,397	30,729
Hakkas	6,170	7,402	8,514
Teochews	22,644	23,737	27,564
Hainanese	8,319	8,711	9,451
Straits-born	9,527	12,805	15,498
Total	86,766	121,908	164,041

Even more important, the dialect groups were mixed residentially and occupationally. A particular dialect group in town was not confined to a particular area but lived with other dialect groups, though the proportions of the ingredients might vary.[12] Even the rural areas which once had an overwhelming number of Teochews were by now quite mixed, with the Hokkiens having a slight edge. These two constraints figured powerfully in the debate, as will be seen.

One alternative the British had was to use the Kapitan China system. This involved the state appointing a Chinese headman over the Chinese, or headmen over wards of Chinese if they were a large population. Where needed, the headmen were allowed one or more assistants or lieutenants. The headmen were subordinate to the magistrates, primarily Europeans, who in turn were appointed by the state.

The purpose of the headman was to exercise what may generally be called a police function over the Chinese, for which the state empowered him to settle and adjust disputes. More serious cases were to be handed over to the magistrate.[13] He had also to register the Chinese, as it facilitated policing. As his reward, he was given certain business privileges such as farm rights, and his social prestige was to some extent enhanced by his association with officialdom. In this scheme of things there was no place for organizations such as the secret societies.

One powerful argument for this system was that it worked elsewhere in South-East Asia and in Hong Kong, and it was not unlike the traditional Chinese system. W. H. Read, a European in Singapore, agreed with a Hong Kong Commission on a headman system, which said that the British 'should use the Chinese system against them', and added that 'the whole police system in China . . . is that of the responsibility of the Elders, and the plan works very successfully. Chinese always arrest their criminals through the Ti-po (i.e. local chief), and we through the elders.'[14]

Despite some reservations in the press that the system might have the effect of uniting rather than dividing the Chinese (the headman system might strengthen the Chinese and then fall under the influence of the secret societies),[15] the basic reason for its rejection was that it would not work.

First, the fluidity and the constant increase of the Chinese population made registration difficult, let alone actual policing. For both to succeed, certain steps had to be taken to restrain movement, with all their adverse consequences for a flexible labour supply. Such a system worked in Java for example because there was an indigenous labour supply,[16] and the Dutch were thus not entirely dependent on the Chinese. Moreover, the Chinese there were few in number and confined to certain quarters.

Second, even assuming that the headman had authority or legitimacy over his particular dialect group, he most surely had none over the other dialect groups. Unless the drastic expedient was adopted of forcing a particular dialect group into one particular territory, a most arduous undertaking, something better had to be tried. William Jervois, the governor, pointed out that in Hong Kong, where a variant of this system was successfully practised, the majority of the population was Cantonese, and thus the problem did not arise.[17]

As to the relevance of the 'traditions of China' argument, some good recent studies[18] on traditional local Chinese society, particularly its relation with the imperial government, allow for some pertinent observations. Crucial to the linkage of bureaucracy and society were the Chinese gentry. Through the mechanism of the clan or lineage—which Maurice Freedman observed was not necessarily the family writ large[19]—the gentry exerted authority over their humbler fellows. Because they came from the same class or group as those in the bureaucracy, which was primarily recruited from the gentry, they either had calling rights with the local magistrate (lesser men had none) or could call the magistrate a friend. The gentry were thus strategically placed to smooth over any difficulties that might arise between bureaucracy and society. Such a group, with credibility on both sides, was precisely what was lacking in Singapore. The Malacca Chinese had it with the British, but not with the population of the residual economy. Consequently, the second alternative of relying on the secret societies to govern the Chinese was proposed and tried.

This policy rested on two assumptions: that the secret societies were in control of the Chinese and that they would co-operate. The first was firmly held by Pickering, the most knowledgeable British officer. If 'secret societies were abolished,' Pickering wrote, 'we should have no check at all on the thousands of the disorderly class of Chinese.'[20] He was not alone in holding this view.[21] The second saw no conflict between the aims of the secret societies and those of the entrepôt society. Where conflict had occurred before, the reasons advanced were either the criminal aspect of the societies, or governmental oppression of the Chinese. Now if the 'political' side of the activities of the societies were not provoked, the criminal side could be kept in check by the ordinances of 1869 and 1877. Pickering himself seemed to be thinking along these lines when he said in 1878 that the societies were criminal and not political in nature,[22] and, if handled properly, could be made to co-operate. He attempted to drive home his argument by suggesting that the government had no alternative, unless it promulgated 'exceptional and more stringent legislation for an exceptional population'.[23] Presumably Pickering meant that in the vacuum created by the abolition of the secret societies the government would have to intervene on a massive scale, creating a policing bureaucracy far bigger than that allowed for in the Chinese Protectorate, and promulgate legislation which would hamper free movement of immigrants in order to ensure some control. The latter would militate against the effective functioning of Singapore as a centre for the distribution of immigrants.

The government saw the force of Pickering's arguments and tried to use the secret societies for a while. Evidently it partially succeeded, for it was stated in one government report that the leaders of the secret societies were co-operating. But it could only be a temporary solution, for the secret societies co-operated, or did not become 'political', only because the government did not basically tamper with the organization of Chinese society. However, this was something the government could not refrain from doing for long. The town had to function efficiently. Moreover, the government had to ensure that there was a supply of satisfactory domestic servants for the European population. There was general dissatisfaction among the European population over this, for the secret societies controlled the distribution of domestic servants, and very often produced servants which was not satisfactory so far as the Europeans were concerned. Any action on these two problems would surely be a challenge to the control of the population of the residual economy by the secret societies, something which should be clear from our analysis of the relationship between the secret societies and this population in previous chapters. The secret societies would then resist or become 'political'.

However in the late 1880s the government decided that they no longer needed the co-operation of the secret societies, and in 1888 they attempted to force hawkers and vendors off the streets in order to prevent cluttering, and to take away the power of the secret societies to control the distribution of servants. Sure enough, the secret societies organized riots in protest. This gave the government the excuse to proscribe them. In 1890 it enacted an ordinance to make it unlawful for 'dangerous' societies to exist or to be formed. Registration would be denied to such associations, and appropriate action would be taken if the regulation were flouted.

This brings us to the alternative the government adopted after 1890, the substitution of these 'dangerous' or secret societies by 'friendly' societies, and the establishment of a Chinese Advisory Board, consisting of prominent Chinese, to act as intermediaries between the government and Chinese society. These 'friendly' societies, which were to perform functions of a charitable nature and thus to keep the Chinese of the residual economy quiescent, appeared in various forms; some were philanthropic in aim, others were cultural, and many were straight forward dialect group associations. It is likely that many, if not all the cultural and other associations, drew the majority of their membership from one particular dialect group. The dialect group nature of these 'friendly' societies can be seen from an examination of the societies considered lawful by the government from 1889 to 1890.

The hui-kuan constituted slightly less than half of all the societies registered, but had the most members. The other societies, from what we know of the predominant absence of organizations cutting across the dialect groups in this period save for the secret societies, probably had memberships strongly represented by members of one dialect group. Notice also the strong representation among the headmen or leaders of these societies of those in the mercantile, clerical, and manufacturing pursuits. The first two groups would have been people more amenable to European influence (the clerks were probably employed by European firms). Thus, there seems to have been a deliberate attempt by the government to encourage organizations led by merchants and dialect group organizations to arise.[25]

This was the solution the British essentially adopted, and it worked. But it must not be assumed that only legislation did the trick. However draconic, legislation would not have been wholly effective had it not been buttressed by favourable social developments. On this score, the British had to ensure two other things; that the secret societies were no longer an important social force, and that there was no difficulty between the Teochew financiers and the Malacca Chinese. Both were made possible by developments in Singapore after intervention. The secret societies became socially irrelevant with the decline of the pioneer nature of the economy. Singapore was now the economic centre of the Malay Peninsula, and given the small size of the island, there was simply

TABLE IX

SOCIETIES REGISTERED IN SINGAPORE UNDER THE SOCIETIES ORDINANCE OF 1889

Name of Society	Principal Headmen	Occupation	Number of members in Registry
1. The Straits Settlements Association	A. Donaldson C. Stringer	Paterson Simons & Co.	114
2. Tiang Ho Sok	Chan Wan Kong	Trader	17
3. Kong Chan Wui Koon [D]	Yong Teng San	Chop 'Kwong Lan'*	45
4. Mutual Philanthropic Association	Chua Bun Wan	Clerk	18
5. Kim Gi	Go Swee Beng	Clerk	39
6. Nam Sun Chan Chak Khoon	Ch'an Kuan Ho	Trader	unknown
7. Cheow Cha Yong Hoe Kwan [D]	Hon Chin Sin	Shopkeeper	299
8. Thung Fuk She	Cheung Seng Chi Cheong Pun Tang San Lan Sam	Watchmaker Shoemaker Shoemaker Shoemaker	61
9. Liong Tek Hoe	Ui Teng Cheow	Merchant	24
10. Ning Yeung Wui Koon [D]	Wong A Fuk	Merchant	254
11. Sui Pi Lin	Sih Guan Liong	Shop Assistant	18
12. Ngo Shang Fui Koon [D]	Liu Ngi Fook	Lodging-House Keeper	157
13. Pak Seng Hong	Chan Yeng	Sundry Shop Keeper	58
14. Tong On Wui Koon [D]	Ng Hong Tai	Lodging-House Keeper	372
15. Ku Seng Wui Koon [D]	Kuan Yok Cheung Hong Fong Lau Nan Keng Chin Kuan Seng	Baker Shopkeeper Contractor Goldsmith	62

*Presumably a trader

No.	Society	Name	Occupation	Number
16.	Kiu Liong Tong	Lim Tong Su	Trader	unknown
17.	Sui Heng Wui Koon [D]	Yam Yun Sun	Bookbinder	139
18.	Ying Fo Fui Koon [D]	Vong Tet Sin	Lodging-House Keeper	566
19.	Po Seng Tai Tei	Tin Ki	Rice Shopkeeper	97
20.	Keng Tak Hong	Man Kuong	Boilermaker	345
21.	Hiong San Wui Koon [D]	Cheung Chun Tin	Dentist	142
22.	Kang He Tong	Ui Seh Chip	Clerk	unknown
23.	Nam Sim Wui Koon [D]	Au Yu Theng	Warehouseman	69
24.	Lu Pak Hoong	Ma A On	Carpenter	84
25.	Hun Kui Tong	Chan Bu Yi	Landowner	12
26.	Eng Chun Hoe Kuan [D]	Li Cheng Yan / Tan Siak Kim	Merchant	unknown
27.	Hokkien Hoe Kuan [D]	Ko San Ti	Trader	unknown
28.	Pun Yu Wui Koon [D]	Tam Hi Fun	Baker	217
29.	Kin Ho	Tan Chun Eng	Cashier	30
30.	Sim Nam Hap	Din Tek / Ho She Wai	Lemonade Manufacturers	186
31.	Lu Seng Hong	Wong Lin Tai	Shipbuilder	86
32.	Kheng Tek Lau	Ang Kim Ti	Merchant	27
33.	Sun Tek Hoe	Go Chiang Kiat	Shopkeeper	32
34.	Tin Bu Bio	Tan Eng Tuan	Shopkeeper	46
35.	Kwong Ngi	Chan A Liong	Boy	74
36.	Gek Ong Siang Te	Ho A Peng	Shipbuilder	75
37.	Kheng Chiu Hoe Kuan [D]	Han Kui Hong	Draper	111

Note: The [D] is the author's addition. It indicates that the society marked with this bracket is a *hui-kuan* (spelled variously here primarily because the term *hui-kuan* is pronounced differently in the various dialects and romanized accordingly), an organization with an explicit dialect group basis.

no room for commercial agriculture on a large scale. Thus, by the 1900s, gambier ceased to be of any importance,[26] while its significance in the Singapore economy had declined even earlier. Second, because there was a constant demand for labour in the peninsula after the 1870s, the migrants who first arrived in Singapore were moved elsewhere. Hence a particular 'surplus' population was unlikely to exist for long in Singapore. Those who remained were more and more likely to have more settled jobs. One indication of a settled population is, of course, the presence of females. It is an indication because only those not involved in pioneer work and only those whose jobs allowed for some permanence and money would be willing and able to send for their wives from China. The figures for the sex ratio should bear out the fact that the Chinese were more settled after the 1870s. Here the figures are added to those produced in the third chapter, the years range from 1824 to 1931.

TABLE X

APPROXIMATE SEX RATIO OF THE CHINESE IN SINGAPORE[27]

Year	Ratio
1824	8.2
1830	11.3
1836	14.6
1849	11.5
1860	14.4
1871	6.2
1881	5.1
1891	4.7
1901	3.9
1911	2.8
1921	2.1
1931	1.7

From the 1860s onwards there was an appreciable decrease in the number of males per female. One possible explanation of this is the Manchu relaxation of the ban on emigration in 1860, which could have encouraged Chinese females to emigrate. But the significance of the figures lies in the trend. That more and more Chinese females were attracted to Singapore would indicate that the intervention must have produced conditions conducive to a more settled existence for the Chinese population. Another indicator would be the existence of schools. For much of the nineteenth century, Chinese schools in Singapore were few and far between whereas they could be counted in the hundreds in the early twentieth century.

The significance of this is that after the 1870s, the 'natural' organizations such as the dialect group associations and the clans, because of the presence of more families, began to assert themselves. One indication of this can be seen from the figures. Thus the authoritative *Hsing-chou shih-nien* in 1940 listed eighty dialect group associations.[28] About ten were established before the 1870s.[29] The equally authoritative *Nan-yang nien-chien* listed the establishment of twenty clans before the Second World War. To the writer's knowledge, only two were formally established before 1870.[30] There is then a correlation between the blooming of the dialect group associations and clans and a more settled population. We shall discuss the social significance of these associations in the next chapter. Here we need only explain why the secret societies lost out.

In Chapter III, we gave as one reason for the early predominance of the secret societies, their use of violence. Now that they were proscribed, their violence could only be used covertly, and was therefore less effective. Chinese who might be threatened for joining the dialect associations could appeal to the British, who were now interested in seeing the dialect group associations flourish. But the other more important reason, the 'social' reason, was their ability to induce a sense of brotherhood and family. As analysed previously, this was accomplished, in addition to force, by elaborate ceremonies. Such ceremonies were effective because they answered the psychological needs of the immigrants, alone in an unknown island far removed from their families in China and probably also without friends, given the involuntary circumstances in which many came. The uncharitable European observer quoted in Chapter III on the efficacy of secret society ceremony on the superstitious Chinese implied that the ceremonies met psychological needs for brotherhood. The growth of Chinese families lessened this secret society role. Whatever welfare functions the secret societies performed could now increasingly be taken care of by the dialect associations and the clans.

There remains the 'political' role of the secret societies, that is, their ability to transcend dialect group divisions either to regulate Chinese society or to meet an external threat. This role was taken over by the Chinese Advisory Board, whose membership was overwhelmingly mercantile. We may consider the year 1890, when the Board was first established, up to 1940.[31] Because the British consistently allowed many members long periods of tenure, we need only to examine those members who served for more than ten years, without fear of excluding the most representative.

These together with their occupations and dialect groups are listed below:

Tan Jiak Kim	Merchant	Hokkien
Lee Cheng Yan	,,	,,
Seah Liang Seah	,,	Teochew
Tan Yong Siak	,,	,,
Lim Boon Keng	Medical doctor and merchant	Hokkien
Go Sin Kho	Merchant	,,
Lim Ho Pua	,,	,,
Lim Sam	,,	,,
Liong Mann Sau	,,	Cantonese
Ng Kwai Pho	No information	,,
Tchan Chun Fook	Merchant	,,
Wee Kim Yam	,,	Teochew
Yau Ngan Pan	,,	Cantonese
Lau Chiang Yi	,,	Teochew
Han Kui Phong	No information	Hainanese
Ui Chian Keng	,,	Hokkien
See Teong Wah	Merchant	,,
Tan Sian-Cheng	,,	,,
Ng Sing Phang	,,	Cantonese
Liau Chia Hing	,,	Teochew
Seah Eng Tong	,,	,,
Thong Siong Lim	High-class tailor and general outfitter	Hakka
Tan Khye Kok	Merchant	Hainanese
Chu Peck Lian	No information	Foochow
Cheong Kee Sun	Merchant	Cantonese
Lee Wee Nam	,,	Teochew
Lim Boon Thim	,,	Cantonese

The British now relied on the merchants to replace the secret societies, and these merchants were deliberately chosen with a view to giving representation to the various dialect groups. Thus Hokkien and Teochew merchants sat on the same board. Given the history of hostility between these two groups, this was an astonishing development. That they were able to co-operate was essentially a result of the economic expansion brought about by the intervention as will be seen in the next chapter.

1. The 'adviser' was a British resident in a state of the peninsula who was supposed to give advice to the Sultan on all things except those touching Malay customs and religion. In practice, like all other façades of indirect rule in South-East Asia, the adviser exercised real political control.

2. See Keith Sinclair, 'Hobson and Lenin in Johore: Colonial Office Policy Towards British Concessionaires and Investors, 1878-1907', *Modern Asian Studies*, 1, No. 4 (1967). Though not exactly writing in the spirit that any follower of Lenin would, Sinclair nevertheless brought out the economic element in British policy.

3. C. N. Parkinson, *British Intervention in Malaya, 1867-1877* (Singapore, University of Malaya Press, 1960); C. D. Cowan, *Nineteenth Century Malaya, the Origins of British Control* (London, Oxford University Press, 1961).

4. See D. R. Sardesai, *Trade and Empire in Malaya and Singapore 1869-1874* (Athens, Ohio University, Center for International Studies, 1970).

5. Khoo Kay Kim, *The Western Malay States 1850-1873; the Effects of Commercial Developments on Malay Politics* (Kuala Lumpur, Oxford University Press, 1972). See also a review of this book by Chris Gray in the *Journal of Asian Studies*, Vol. XXXII, No. 3, May 1973, pp.557-8.

6. An example of independent Chinese economic activity is their investment in gambier and pepper in Johore before the 1870s. But even before this, there was a time when the British had to use their political influence with the Sultan of Johore when the latter was involved with the Chinese merchants in Singapore. The British intervened on the side of the Chinese merchants. See C. M. Turnbull, 'The Johore Gambier and Pepper Trade in the mid-19th Century', *Journal of the South Seas Society*, Vol. XV, Part I, 1959.

7. The figures before the 1870s were taken from relevant issues of the *Singapore Free Press*, while after the 1870s they were taken from the *Annual Reports of the Chinese Protectorate*. The 1860s are missing here because no figures could be found from 1855 to 1869.

8. See the 1901 census of the Straits Settlements.

9. It might be that the Chinese Protectorate was a response to local developments (see E. Thio, 'Singapore Chinese Protectorate'). But, while it is true that the functions of the Protectorate were to meet problems arising from a local context, as it should, the point is that the British would not have been concerned had not Singapore figured in a larger scheme. It has to be emphasized that the problems mentioned existed in Singapore well before 1877 without the British government being much concerned.

10. Joyce Ee, 'Chinese Migration to Singapore, 1896-1941', *Journal of Southeast Asian History*, March 1961.

11. Taken from the censuses of the Straits Settlements for the relevant years. The Cantonese from these censuses form a significant portion. This suggests the increasing urbanization of Singapore since they were the dialect group most involved in the activities resulting from an urban environment.

12. In Straits Settlements Records, 13 and 17 May 1854, it was stated that the Teochews, Hokkiens, and Cantonese, lived alongside each other along the same street and in different parts of the town. The missionary Stronach, in his correspondence with London, wrote of visiting places where Teochews and Hokkiens were juxtaposed, 22 August 1839 and 24 September 1841. See also the Straits Settlements census of 1891. In this census, the town was divided into many divisions, and in each division the various dialect groups were mixed. For example, in Division A

there were 7,055 Cantonese, 5,838 Hokkiens, 735 Hainanese, 563 Hakkas and 3,284 Teochews.

13. See Regulation No. III of 1823, dated 20 January 1823 which consolidated much of Raffles' instructions to Bonham *et al.* See also Wong, *A Gallery* and *Singapore Free Press*, 11 August 1854.

14. Wong, op. cit., p.30.

15. Stated by Europeans in Singapore in 1854 and 1855 and, no doubt, held by some in the late nineteenth century. See *Singapore Free Press*, 11 August 1854 and 12 May 1855.

16. Chinese immigration to Java ceased after 1873. See Thio, op. cit.

17. See *Straits Settlements Correspondence*; Governor to Secretary of State, 20 August 1875.

18. For a good study which focuses on local government, see T'ung-Tsu Chu, *Local Government in China under the Ching* (Stanford, Stanford University Press, 1962). For one which focuses on local society but has some treatment on its relationship with the state, see Freedman, *Lineage Organization*. For one which focuses on the Chinese gentry, see Fei Hsiao-Tung, *The Chinese Gentry/Essays in Rural-Urban Relationships*, rev. and ed. by M. P. Redfield (Chicago, University of Chicago Press, 1968).

19. Freedman, *Lineage Organizations*, p.2.

20. See his discussion on the secret societies in *Journal of Royal Asiatic Society*, June 1879, pp.1-18.

21. *Singapore Free Press*, 7 January 1890 for an editorial to this effect.

22. W. A. Pickering, 'Chinese Secret Societies and their Origins', *Journal of Royal Asiatic Society (Straits Branch)* of July 1878-79, p.1.

23. Ibid., p.11.

24. Taken from the *Annual Report of the Chinese Protectorate, 1890*, Singapore

26. Gambier and pepper had already begun to decline from the 1860s onwards though they picked up later. However, by the 1900s they were reduced to insignificance.

27. Taken from Saw Swee Hock, *Singapore Population*, p.60.

28. *Hsing-chou shih-nien, Hsing-chou-yueh-pao shih-chou-nien chi-nien t'e-kan (Ten Years of Singapore, Special Tenth Anniversary Publication of the Hsing-chou-yueh-pao)*, Singapore, 1940, pp.940-4.

29. The eighty associations were checked with the societies list given above to see if dialect group associations were included. Then the dates of establishment of the dialect group associations, those known to be established before 1890, were examined to see how many were established before 1870. There were about ten.

30. *Nan-yang nien-chien* (Singapore, 1951), pp.270-8.

31. Compiled from *Straits Settlements Civil Service Lists*; *Straits Settlements Annual Departmental Reports* (Singapore, Government Printing Press); and *Singapore and Malayan Directory* published by the *Straits Times*. All in the relevant years. Information on the occupations of merchants is taken from other sources.

VI

THE STRUCTURE OF THE CHINESE MERCANTILE CLASS AFTER INTERVENTION

THE hostility between the Malacca Chinese and the Teochews was the result of the encroachment of free trade. But intervention in Malaya was to stop this encroachment and to divert the British to the Malay Peninsula. At the same time intervention opened up economic opportunities for the Chinese merchants, the result of which was to reduce conflict and to change the nature of the Chinese mercantile class. The realization grew among the conflicting merchants that their best interests were to be found more in seizing new economic opportunities in the Malay Peninsula than fighting among themselves in an economy in Singapore which was constant. Those with existing interests should be allowed to retain them, while the expansionary drive of all the merchants could be met in the Peninsula through the specialization of economic functions. In this way there was room for everybody.

This will become clearer when we examine certain characteristics of the Chinese mercantile class after intervention, essentially those who were in the Chinese Chambers of Commerce. The Chambers which was formed in 1906 consisted of the most prominent members of the various dialect groups. It was without doubt the organization *par excellence* of the Chinese merchants in Singapore, as it was elsewhere in South-East Asia.[1] No other Chinese mercantile group in Singapore approached it in size or influence.[2] It is thus possible to assume that from the early twentieth century the Chambers consisted of members who were representative of the Chinese mercantile class. The intention here is to choose a representative group from the membership of the Chambers, it being too tedious and time-consuming to treat every single member, and array their characteristics relevant to our analysis. Names which appear on the Committees of the Chambers for more than five periods have been selected from the available lists. The number is arbitrarily chosen, but is long enough to catch those who were the most influential. The number came to forty-six.[3] Of this number, we have information for thirty-five.

The following characteristics will be listed: the year and place of birth; the dialect group; the inheritance, which essentially involved the circumstances in which they started in Singapore; the presence of a tertiary education; the existence of business involvement in Malaya; and the existence of involvement in China in, e.g., charity, investment, work, and political activities.

The list appears on pages 101 to 106.

This list basically confirms the specialization of economic functions. The Hokkiens are strongly represented in shipping, insurance, banking, and rubber (there is some Teochew representation in banking and rubber but not so strong; the Hokkiens had three banks to one Teochew before 1930).[4] This is not surprising, given the capital involved and the political influence necessary, for the Hokkiens, being the best-established group, possessed these two items in greater degree than the others. Thus a Chinese observer in 1878 mentioned that the Hokkien merchants invested much more capital in shipping than merchants in other businesses.[5] On the other hand, the Teochews maintained their hold on whatever gambier and pepper agriculture—which the same observer mentioned needed less capital than shipping and banking—was left. No merchant from any other dialect group in this list was involved in gambier and pepper agriculture. Hence this agriculture, together with local produce, piece-goods, remittance, and the cloth business, because of the lesser capital involved and the greater need for the management of labour, predictably found strong Teochew representation.[6] The other dialect groups, thinly represented because of the smallness of their numbers and businesses, did well in the crafts in which they had been long established. (One, Li Leung Ki in the insurance business and listed as a Cantonese, associated primarily with Hokkiens and was often considered as such.)[7] Thus the economic specialization of the various dialect groups dovetailed in quite neatly with the expanding pie, or rather, it was apportioned well.

Finally, the overwhelming majority of the merchants in this list were involved in business in the Malay Peninsula, thus adding to the argument that they took advantage of the economic opportunities there.

TABLE XI

BIRTHPLACE AND OTHER CHARACTERISTICS OF 35 CHINESE WHO
SERVED FOR MORE THAN FIVE PERIODS ON THE COMMITTEE OF
THE SINGAPORE CHINESE CHAMBERS OF COMMERCE BETWEEN 1906 AND 1941

Name	Place and Year of Birth	Dialect Group	Inheritance	Tertiary Education	Occupation	China Involvement	Malaya Involvement
Lim Peng Siang	Amoy, China 1906	Hokkien	Came at an early age	No	Banker; shipping, oil mill, cement, coconut business	Yes	Yes
Lim Boon Keng	Singapore 1869	Hokkien	Educated in Singapore	Received medical degree from University of Edinburgh	Also director of rubber and tin companies; insurance business; and banker	Yes	Yes
Teo Sian Keng	Nan Ching, China	Hokkien	Came to Singapore at 31 years old	No	Merchant	Yes	—
See Teong Wah	Straits 1886	Hokkien	Descendant of famous See family from Malacca	No	Compradore with British bank in Singapore; also in shipping business	—	Yes
See Boo Ih	Enn Meng, China	Hokkien	Came first to Netherlands India at 26 years of age	No	Banker with Hokkien banks; also in rubber business	Yes	Yes
Tan Sian Cheng	China	Hokkien	Came to Singapore at 15 years old	No	Banker in a Hokkien bank	Yes	—

Name	Place and Year of Birth	Dialect Group	Inheritance	Tertiary Education	Occupation	China Involvement	Malaya Involvement
Tan Ean Khiam	Tong Ann, China 1881	Hokkien	Came to Singapore at 18 years old	No	Rubber, insurance, biscuit, and sawmill business; also in car transport and banking with Hokkien banks	Yes	Yes
Chua Kah Cheong	China	Hokkien	Came to Singapore at 22 years old	No	Banker	—	—
Lee Choon Seng	Eng Choon, China 1888	Hokkien	Came to Singapore at 19 years old	No	Biscuit, insurance and rubber business; banker with Hokkien banks	Yes	Yes
Lee Chin Tian	Theng Hai, China	Hokkien	Came first to Sarawak, then later to Singapore	No	Rubber, local produce and sundry goods business	Yes	Yes
Yap Twee	—	Hokkien	—	—	Insurance, building materials and hardware business; leading banker in Hokkien banks	—	—

Name	Place and Year of Birth	Dialect Group	Inheritance	Tertiary Education	Occupation	China Involvement	Malaya Involvement
Lee Kim Soon	Straits	Hokkien	Ancestors came from Malacca	No	Cement and other materials needed for the building trade; banking	—	—
Lee Kong Chian	Nan Ann, China 1894	Hokkien	Came to Singapore at 10 years old	Went to a communications university in Shanghai	First teacher and surveyor with the municipality; then in rubber produce, sawmill, pineapple, realty-insurance business; also a banker with Hokkien banks	Yes	Yes
Lim Kin Tian	Tong Ann, China	Hokkien	Came to Singapore at 13 years old	No	Owner of lighters in the shipping business	—	—
Lim Keng Lian	Ann Khoey, China	Hokkien	Tea business started by father in Amoy, then extended to Singapore	Attended Peking University	Tea business; also in remittance business; banker with a Hokkien bank	Yes	Yes
Gan Say Hong	Tong Ann, China	Hokkien	Came to Singapore at 16 years old	No	Banker with Hokkien banks; local produce and fish business	Yes	Yes

Name	Place and Year of Birth	Dialect Group	Inheritance	Tertiary Education	Occupation	China Involvement	Malaya Involvement
Ong Piah Teng	Quemoy, China 1892	Hokkien	Came to Singapore at one year old	No	Banker with Hokkien banks; importer and exporter of ship chandlery, ropes, cotton ducks	Yes	Yes
Tan Teck Joon	Chao Aun, China 1859	Teochew	Came to Singapore in early years	No	Cloth, piece-goods merchant; importer and exporter; banker with Four Seas Bank	—	Yes
Chua Tsz Yong	Theng Hai, China 1846	Teochew	Came to Singapore by way of extending his business in China	No	Medicine, piece-goods, silk, sugar, and rice merchant	—	—
Liau Chia Heng	Chao Aun, China 1874	Teochew	Came to Singapore at an early age	No	Gambier and pepper, local produce and cloth merchant, importer and exporter, banker with Four Seas Bank	Yes	Yes
Heng Pang Kiat	Chao Aun, China 1885	Teochew	Came to Singapore at 16 years old	No	Cloth merchant, has a remittance shop; insurance	Yes	Yes

Name	Place and Year of Birth	Dialect Group	Inheritance	Tertiary Education	Occupation	China Involvement	Malaya Involvement
Yeo Chang Boon	Chao Aun, China 1881	Teochew	Came to Singapore at an early age	No	Cloth, local produce merchant	Yes	Yes
Tan Jiak Ngoh	Chao Aun, China 1866	Teochew	Son of Tan Yong Siak; inherited much from father	No	Oil mill owner, owned remittance shop; commission agent	Yes	Yes
Lim Nee Soon	Singapore 1879	Teochew	Father a small trader	No	Rubber business; contractor, general commission agent; pineapple business	Yes	Yes
Teo Eng Hock	Jao Ping, China	Teochew	—	No	Not very successful cloth merchant; mainly involved in newspapers and literary publications to promote KMT causes	Yes	Yes
Lee Wee Nam	Theng Hai, China 1881	Teochew	Came to Singapore at 16 years old	No	Banker with Four Seas Bank; owner of two remittance shops; importer and exporter	Yes	Yes
Tan Keng T'ng	Chao Aun, China 1856	Teochew	Succeeded to father's business	No	Gambier and pepper and local produce merchant	Yes	Yes
Ng Sing Phang	En-Ping, China	Cantonese	Came at 21 years old to Singapore	No	Timber business	—	—

Name	Place and Year of Birth	Dialect Group	Inheritance	Tertiary Education	Occupation	China Involvement	Malaya Involvement
Loke Yan Kit	Canton, China 1849	Cantonese	Practised dentistry first in Japan and Hongkong, then came to Singapore	Yes	Dentist and landlord	Yes	—
Lam Boon Thin	Ning Yang, China	Cantonese	Came at 16 to Singapore	No	Pawnshop business	Yes	—
Li Leung Ki	Tai Shan, China	Cantonese	Came to Singapore at age of 20	No	Insurance business	Yes	—
S. Q. Wong	Singapore	Cantonese	Inherited business from father	Yes	First lawyer, then gave up to do business in rubber, tin, cars, insurance, rent, bank	Yes	Yes
Chin Yong Kwong	Singapore	Hakka	Inherited father's business with Borneo	—	Merchant	—	—
Thong Siong Lim	Singapore	Hakka	—	No	High-class tailor and outfitter	—	—
Aw Boon Haw	Rangoon, Burma	Hakka	Succeeded to father's modest business	No	Manufacturer of medicinal products; owner of newspapers; and banker with Hakka bank	Yes	Yes
Tan Khye Kok	—	Hainanese	—	—	Merchant	—	—

One other fact that needs explanation is the apparent absence of the Malacca Chinese in this list, or at least there was none born in Malacca, though some might have been descended from them. One reason lies in the rise of the compradore class in China, which began after 1842 when Hong Kong was acquired by the British, and was given a further impetus when more treaty ports were opened on the Yangtze and the northern China coast in 1860. The compradore was a Chinese merchant who essentially acted as a middleman between the Western merchants and the Chinese in China, and would therefore have developed those skills and assets needed for the proper conduct of business with the Europeans. Many compradores in China were Cantonese. There can be no doubt that they extended their influence to the Chinese in Singapore, if not by actually migrating to Singapore then at least by extending their business contacts there. Thus Hao Yen-Ping, in his book on the comprador in China, quoted an American merchant, Thomas Know, as writing in 1878 that the Chinese compradore was active in Japan, Cochin China, Bangkok, Rangoon, Penang, Malacca, Singapore, Java, and Manila, and that his influence was even felt in India. This meant that within Singapore itself, by the time of the British intervention in Malaya, there would be many non-Malacca Chinese who could deal with the British just as the Malacca Chinese did. This would reduce British dependence on the Malacca Chinese.[8]

The second reason was the change in the nature of the economy after intervention, where previously the entrepôt economy depended chiefly on the straight exchange of European goods and native produce, it was now enlarged to include those activities needed to service enterprises where great numbers of Chinese were involved. There are no precise figures as to the size of this enlargement, but it must have been very great. This can be seen from the list which shows that the predominant pursuits of the merchants were in shipping, banking, insurance, rubber, tin, and gambier and pepper. As most of these, if not all, involved large numbers of Chinese labourers primarily from China, the Malacca Chinese would not be able to manage them as well as the China-born Chinese could.

Nevertheless, they could have coped with this new situation in two ways. First, they could have started some of these enterprises and used their own kind for labour. This was, however, not possible because there were not enough of them. For example, the

Malacca Chinese population in 1860 was given as 10,039.[9] Even assuming that all the Chinese there were willing to work as coolies, a most unlikely assumption, their numbers would be nothing compared to the hundreds of thousands of Chinese who came from China. Moreover, many lacked the pioneering spirit, something commented on by observers who stated that many successful Malacca Chinese tended to return to Malacca and become idle,[10] which was lamented by some of their own people when compared to the more vigorous immigrants from China.[11]

Second, they could have absorbed the successful Chinese migrants. Maurice Freedman stated that this may have been the case in the nineteenth century, and suggested that their marriage system could have been helpful.[12] In such a system, while the children stayed with the mother and her parents, the rights of the father were not prejudiced. The children still bore his surname. But in practice the children came under the influence of the maternal grandparents and thus could be useful for keeping the successful immigrant son-in-law in line. (We have some evidence in Chapter II for this.) But there were limits. The Chinese population from China simply grew too large for the Malacca Chinese to control and this system could not be sustained for long. Certainly, the great social instability during that period does suggest some breakdown in Malacca Chinese assimilation of successful migrants.

Thus, there were only two realistic alternatives open to the Malacca Chinese. The first was to enter those businesses for which much capital and skill (in the sense of technical ability such as accounting) were needed, businesses such as shipping and banking. Some did this. In the list of Hokkien merchants, three, Lim Peng Siang, See Teong Wah and Lee Kim Soon, were descendants of Malacca Chinese (Lim Peng Siang was descended on his maternal side from Kong Tuan and Choa Chong Long) while the fourth, Lim Boon Keng, had many associations with them. Those born in Singapore from the other dialect groups on the list had fathers who originated from China. These four were found in either banking or shipping or in both.[13] Moreover capital-intensive businesses were dominated by the Hokkiens and the Malacca Chinese could identify with them.

A second alternative was open to children of established wealth in an immigrant society should they not follow their fathers' path of business in public life. But Singapore was then a colonial society with political power and the upper echelons of the bureaucracy the firm preserve of the British. The Chinese were excluded, except for the very, very few who might be appointed as unofficial members in the legislature.[14] Hence the only positions left were the minor rungs of the bureaucracy, such as the clerical services which the British disdained, and the professions, such as law and medicine. It is not surprising that many Malacca Chinese crept into such clerical services because of their skill in the English language and their good relationship with the British. Nor is it surprising that they entered the professions, since they possessed the wealth and the language ability to allow for the necessary education in English universities.

An examination of the rate of tertiary education among the Chairmen of the Straits Chinese-British Association should show this interest in the professions. Many of the Straits Chinese were descended from Malacca Chinese and all were born in the Straits Settlements. Therefore they would form a good indication of the occupations pursued by children of successful immigrants in Singapore. The Straits Chinese-British Association was, as the name implies, an association of Chinese who were born in the Straits Settlements.

TABLE XII

THE LEADERSHIP OF THE STRAITS CHINESE-BRITISH ASSOCIATION
1900–1941 ACCORDING TO EARLIEST DATE OF OFFICE[15]

Leaders	Education
Tan Jiak Kim	Private English Education
Seah Liang Seah	Secondary English Education
Lee Choon Guan	Private Education
Lim Boon Keng	Tertiary English Education (medicine)
Song Ong Siang	Tertiary English Education (law)
Wong Siew Qui	,, ,, ,, ,,
Wee Swee Teow	,, ,, ,, ,,
Chan Sze Jin	,, ,, ,, ,,
Lim Han Hoe	Tertiary English Education (medicine)
Tay Lian Teck	Secondary English Education
Ong Tiang Wee	Tertiary English Education (law)

About three-quarters of this sample were people who had professional degrees, very much higher than a comparable percentage of the sample of members of the Chambers. All but one had an English education, either in Singapore or, if tertiary, in an English university, confirming the interest the Malacca Chinese and their descendants had in the professions.

Thus the economic position of the Malacca Chinese had changed somewhat after intervention. The overwhelming domination they had held under free trade gave way to a situation where more enterprising immigrants from China began ruling the economic roost, and where in order to continue maintaining their prosperity, they had to go along with the new economic order. But this did not mean they had also to give way in the political leadership of the Chinese so far as the British were concerned.

1. See Skinner, *Chinese Society*, p.171.

2. Like the Chambers in Thailand, the Chambers in Singapore became the organization representing the Chinese Government. It was formed at the prompting of Chang Pi-shih, representing the Chinese Government, in 1906. A high Chambers official, in an interview, aptly described the prompting as midwifery, the embryo already being developed internally, i.e. when the merchants had reduced their differences. The Chambers were so powerful that the government in China treated them as a sort of *hsien* or district government.

3. The names have been taken from the Straits Times Directory for Singapore and Malaya for the years 1906 to 1941. Apparently the Chinese Chambers of Commerce themselves do not have the names of the committee members for all the years mentioned. Their records consist of the names of all the committee members for the year 1906 and for the years from 1937 to 1941. For the intervening years, the Chambers have only the names of presidents, vice-presidents, and a few prominent members. Presumably, they must have lost the records for the missing years. The names the Chambers have can be found in their publication, the *Economic Monthly*.

The information of those in the sample was obtained in this way. First, the transliteration of the forty-six names from English to Chinese was examined by Mr. Tan Ee Leong, a secretary for many years in the Chambers and who knew some of the members personally. This was then checked with the publications of the Chambers which often have the name of a person both in English and Chinese. Lest the reader be in some doubt as to the necessity of such a step, consider a Chinese name like 陳嘉庚. If pronounced in Mandarin, the English transliteration will be Chen Chia-keng while it will be Tan Kah-kee in Hokkien and Teochew and probably Chin Kah-keng in Hakka and Chan Kah-keng in Cantonese. Now, sometimes the four different English versions might appear in different publications, and the only way the reader can be sure all refer to the same person is to find out the Chinese name. After this, all the available English sources together with most of the Chinese ones were ransacked for information. This was supplemented with some interviews. That relevant information was found only for thirty-five members should reveal the difficulty of ferreting out information from Chinese merchants. The information was obtained from the following sources:
in English:

Song, *One Hundred Years*; Wright and Cartwright (eds.), *Twentieth Century Impressions of British Malaya* (London, Greater Lloyd's Publishing Co., 1908).
in Chinese:

Hsin-chia-po chung-hua-tsung-shang-hui ta hsia lo ch'eng chi-nien-kan (*Souvenir of the Opening Ceremony of the Newly Completed Singapore Chinese Chambers of Commerce Building*), Singapore, 1964; *Hsin-chia-po chung-hua-tsung-shang-hui ch'ing chu tsuan hsi chi-nien-t'e-kan (The Souvenir of the Sixtieth Anniversary of the Singapore Chinese Chambers of Commerce*), Singapore, 1966; *Hsin-chia-po chung-hua-tsung-shang-hui ch'ing-chi-yueh-pao (Economic Monthly: Journal of the Singapore Chinese Chambers of Commerce*), Singapore. Numbers for 10 June 1969; 10 February, 10 March, 10 May, 10 June 1970, 10 May 1971; *Hsin-chia-po ch'a-yang-hui-kuan I pai chou nien chi-nien-t'e-kan (Special Publication of the 100th Anniversary Celebration of the Singapore Ch'a-yang hui-kuan*), Singapore, 1958; *Hsin-chia-po ning-yang-hui-kuan I pai san shih chou nien chi-nien t'e-kan (Special Publication of the 130th Anniversary Celebration of the Singapore Ning-yang-hui-kuan*), Singapore, 1952; *Hsin-chou ying-ho-hui-kuan I pai ssu shih chou nien chi-nien-t'e-kan (Special Publication of the 140th Anniversary Celebration of the Singapore Ying-ho-hui-kuan*), Singapore, 1965; *Lin Po-ai and others, Nan-yang ming-jen chi-chuan (A Collection of Famous Men in South-East Asia*), Penang, 1922; *Lung-hsi-li-shih chi-nien t'e-kan (Special Commemorative Publication of the Lung-hsi-li-shih clan); Nan-an-hui-kuan san shih chou nien chi-nien t'e-kan (Special Publication of the Thirtieth Anniversary Celebration of the Singapore Nan-an-hui kuan*), Singapore, 1949; *Nan-shun-hui-kuan ching tseng (Publication of the Nan-shun-hui-kuan*), Singapore, 1964; *Nan-yang k'e-shu-tsung-hui ti san shih wu lu chou nien chi-nien-kan (35th or 36th Speical Commemorative Publication of the Nanyang Khek Community Guild, Singapore*), Singapore, 1967; P'an Hsing-nung, *Ma-la-ya ch'ao-ch'iao t'ung-chien (The Teochews in Malaya*), Singapore, 1950; Su Hsiao-hsien, *Chang-chou shih-shu lu-hsing t'ung-hsiang-lu (Chronicles of the Residents of Changchou*), Singapore, 1950; Sung Cho-ying, *Hsien-tai tung-nan-ya ch'eng-kung-jen-wu chih (The Successful Men of South-East Asia*), Singapore, 1968; Sung Che-mei, *Hsing-ma jen-wu chih (Who's who in Malaya and Singapore*), Hongkong, 1969; *Yang-shih-chia-p'u (Genealogy of the Yang Clan*), Kuala Lumpur, 1962; and also in personal interviews or discussions with:

a. Mr. Tan Ee Leong, a secretary of the Chinese Chambers of Commerce for many years.

b. Mr. Tan Yoek Seong, a retired businessman and scholar who knew many of the merchants personally.

c. Mr. Lee Yip Lim, now with the *Hsing-chou-yueh-pao*, Kuala Lumpur.

4. See Tan Ee Leong, 'Chinese Banks Incorporated in Singapore and the Federation of Malaya', *Journal of Royal Asiatic Society (Malayan Branch*), Vol. 26, Part 1, July 1953.

5. Li, *A Description of Singapore.*

6. This list of Teochew merchants still involved in the rice and remittance business suggests that the attempt by the British, in alliance with Hokkiens, to encroach on these two businesses was not wholly successful. The explanation for this probably lies in the fact that the British lost out to the Teochews in Thailand. As Skinner described it, the Chinese willingness to work full steam, their extensive contacts within Thailand and their ability to adapt to mechanization enabled them to survive the British onslaught. It would thus seem that the British could not in this respect prevent the continuation of the Teochew supply of rice to Singapore. See Skinner, op. cit., pp.104-5. The fact that a Chinese observer, Li, in 1887, in op. cit., said that Singapore obtained its rice from Siam, Annam, and Burma, can only confirm that the Teochews did not lose out.

7. Information supplied by Mr. Tan Ee Leong.

8. Hao Yen-Ping, *The Comprador in Nineteenth Century China: Bridge between East and West* (Cambridge, Harvard University Press, 1970), p.55.

However, while there may be Chinese compradors from China in Singapore, this in no wise means that the Chinese mercantile class in Singapore which developed after intervention, was comprador in character, not at least in the definition of Wickberg in *The Chinese*, p.79. A comprador in China, Wickberg wrote, was one with three characteristics. He knew a Western language; he operated in a hybrid system where he had a material credit relationship with the Westerners but a personal one with the Chinese, and he was contractually and physically attached to a Western firm. Not all Singapore Chinese merchants possessed these characteristics, especially after the 1930s. But in so far as the term comprador implies subordination to Western capital then it is an accurate description.

9. See Chang, *History of Malacca*, pp.324-32.

10. See 'Notes on the Chinese in the Straits', *Journal of the Indian Archipelago*, Vol. IX, 1855. The author wrote that children of wealthy Malacca Chinese 'tended to dissipate fortunes left by painstaking parents', p.120.

11. *Straits Chinese Magazine*, Vol. 3, No. 11, 1899. See article on Seah Eu Chin. Tan Tek Soon, in 'Chinese Local Trade', *Straits Chinese Magazine*, Vol. VI, March 1902, p.92 wrote of the Babas [descendants of Malacca Chinese] that they were 'by affinity of language, custom and temperament perhaps more fitted for [internal trade in the peninsula than the immigrants], yet they have never seriously attempted to avail themselves of the opportunities offered them. They positively dislike the solitary monotonous existence without any of the usual amenities of civilized life. . . .'

12. See Freedman, 'Immigrants and Associations'. See also his 'Chinese Kinship and Marriage in Early Singapore', *Journal of Southeast Asian History*, University of Singapore, 1962, p.66.

13. In this connexion, one should mention the increasing re-sinification of the Malacca Chinese after the intervention. This should be understandable, for even in shipping and banking some rapport with the Chinese, mainly Hokkiens, was important for business success. After all, many of the clients of the banks were Chinese and the ships would transport goods produced by Chinese labour, not to mention Chinese coolies. In such circumstances the Malacca Chinese would deem it wise to acquire greater 'Chineseness'. Thus the genealogy of the See family from Malacca showed some members of the family going to China to study in the latter half of the nineteenth century. (This genealogy was kindly lent to me by a descendant, Mrs. Lucy Chen, cf. Vaughan, *Manners*, p.16, that Hokkien Babas did not send their children to China to study in 1879. Presumably there was no need to do so before that.) Lim Peng Siang himself was born and educated as a child in China despite his connexions on the maternal side to famous Malacca Chinese like Kong Tuan and Choa Chong Long, and many descendants of Malacca Chinese actually served in the Chinese administration in China. This trend towards re-sinification took on a particularly acute form just after the Second World War when a veritable explosion of Chinese nationalism occurred among the Chinese in Singapore and Malaya. See Freedman's discussion of re-sinification of the overseas Chinese in R. O. Tilman (ed.), *Man, State and Society in Southeast Asia* (New York, Praeger, 1969).

14. See Grace Chia Beng Imm, *Asian Members of the Straits Settlements Legislative Council (1908-1941)*, (B.A. Hons. Academic Exercise), (Singapore, University of Singapore, 1960).

15. Taken from Yong Ching Fatt, 'A Preliminary Study of Chinese Leadership in Singapore 1900-1941', in the *Journal of Southeast Asian History*, Vol. 9, No. 2 (September 1968).

VII

POSTSCRIPT

THE preceding chapters have shown how Chinese society in Singapore was basically determined by the operation of the international economy and the changes in it. Under free trade a mercantile class was created which had little control over Chinese society, while the latter responded to free trade essentially by organizing itself into secret societies. This had great potential for violence, which was duly realized when the full consequences of free trade were felt. The violence was only overcome when free trade was replaced by a policy of colonialism in the Malay Peninsula, a policy which linked Singapore politically to the peninsula and opened vast economic opportunities. This policy also led to a change in the composition in the mercantile class, in which a more Chinese group replaced the Malacca Chinese. Meanwhile, the secret societies were proscribed. At the same time, the new mercantile class was able to draw closer to Chinese society to some extent by its domination of the dialect group associations and the clans, which increasingly replaced the secret societies. It remains to show the effect of that cataclysmic development in the international economy in the 1920s and 1930s, the Depression, on the Chinese mercantile class; and how it brought this class some limited autonomy from the British.

The catastrophic 1920s slump in the prices of tin and rubber, the two mainstays of the Malayan economy, together with the restrictions placed by the colonial government on the amount of tin and rubber which could be exported from Malaya and Singapore (restrictions which were to work in favour of the European mercantile community) were to bankrupt many Chinese merchants.[1] Many came to realize that they were particularly vulnerable if they were to depend entirely on the import and export trade between the West and South-East Asia. Consequently, they sought more secure outlets for their investments. They found them in what may be called nationally-based businesses, i.e., those not directly dependent on the import and export trade. Examples were real estate and light consumer industries. This is shown by repeating part of the list of the Chinese Chambers of Commerce members given in Chapter V, with the addition of the year in which the members first entered the Chambers:

TABLE XIII
FIRST YEAR OF MEMBERSHIP OF CHINESE CHAMBERS OF COMMERCE AND OCCUPATION OF 35 MERCHANTS

Name	First Year of Membership of Chambers	Occupation
Lim Peng Siang	1906	banking, shipping, parboiled rice, oil mill, cement, coconut business
Lim Boon Keng	1906	rubber, tin, insurance, and banking business
Teo Sian Keng	1906	merchant
Tan Teck Joon	1906	cloth, piece-goods, and banking business; also an importer and exporter
Chua Tsz Yong	1906	medicine, piece-goods, silk, sugar, and rice business
Liau Chia Heng	1906	gambier and pepper, local produce, cloth, and banking business, also an importer and exporter
Heng Pang Kiat	1906	cloth, remittance, and insurance business
Chin Yong Kwong	1906	merchant
Yeo Chang Boon	1906	cloth, local produce business
See Teong Wah	1909	comprador with British bank; also in rubber business
Tan Sian Cheng	1909	banking business
See Boo Ih	1914	rubber, and banking business
Tan Jiak Ngoh	1918	oil mill, remittance and commission business
Tan Ean Khiam	1920	rubber, insurance, biscuit, sawmill, car transport, and banking business
Ng Sing Phang	1920	timber business
Loke Yan Kit	1922	dentist and landlord
S. Q. Wong	1922	rubber, tin, car, insurance, rent and banking business

Thong Siong Lim	1922	high-class tailor and outfitter
Tan Khye Kok	1922	merchant
Lim Nee Soon	1922	rubber, contractor, pineapple, and general commission business
Tan Keng T'ng	1922	gambier and pepper, and local produce business
Chua Kah Cheong	1924	banking business
Teo Eng Hock	1924	cloth merchant; involved in newspapers and other literary publications to promote the KMT cause
Lim Kim Tian	1926	owner of lighters in shipping business
Lee Wee Nam	1926	banking, remittance, and import and export business
Lee Kong Chian	1928	rubber, local produce, sawmill, pineapple, realty, insurance, and banking business
Lee Kim Soon	1928	cement and materials used in the building business
Lee Choon Seng	1928	biscuit, rubber, and banking business
Li Leung Ki	1930	insurance business
Aw Boon Haw	1931	medicinal products, manufacturer, owner of newspapers, and banker
Lee Chin Tian	1932	rubber, local produce, and piece-goods business
Yap Twee	1932	building materials, hardware, and banking business
Lim Keng Kian	1932	tea, remittance and banking business
Gan Say Hong	1934	banking, local produce and fish business
Lim Boon Thin	1935	pawnshop business

If we consider those merchants who first began as Chambers' members in 1928 (about the time the prices of tin and rubber slumped) and after, it seems that practically all had some involvement in a nationally-based business such as the manufacture of medicinal products, biscuits, cement and building materials, in dealings in local produce, piece-goods, cloth, and real estate, and in services like the remittance (to China, that is, and therefore independent of the Western import and export trade) and pawnshop business. Compare these men to the pre-1928 members, especially those joining in the 1900s and the 1910s; these merchants were very strong in tin, rubber, gambier and pepper, silk, sugar, rice, and other products which were dependent on the Westernized import and export sector. This is not to say that the Chinese mercantile class totally changed after the Depression and became what may be called a national mercantile class. Basically they did not, as the post-1928 list, still showing strong representation of rubber, pine-apple, and banking businesses, would indicate. Moreover, any change in investment patterns took some time to be fully felt, often much more than ten years.   . .

But a change there was. And if it did not allow for total independ-ence from the Western-dominated international economy, it allowed for some. This partial independence was bound to have political implications, for many of the more independent merchants were emboldened to embark on activities not entirely looked upon with favour by the British, activities such as active involvement in nationalistic and anti-British activities in China and resistance to unfavourable British policies towards the Chinese in Malaya and Singapore. While this might not have shattered stability, it did mean that the British had more difficulty than before in controlling the merchants.

The best way of demonstrating this partial independence is to examine a representative sample of members of the Chinese Advisory Board before the Depression, say before 1930, and com-pare it with a representative sample after 1930. For the pre-1930 sample, we choose those members who had been on the Board for ten years and more, and in the post-1930 list, those who had been on the Board for seven or more years between 1930 and 1940. The information provided is relevant to a judgement as to whether a member was more 'Chinese' than the others, it being assumed that if the British had total control they would choose those mer-chants who were more Westernized and less 'Chinese'. This can be seen in Tables XIV and XV.

From Table XIV we can see that practically everyone had some characteristics which the Europeans would look upon with favour, characteristics such as birth in the Straits Settlements, ties with the Malacca Chinese, and an English education. All were basically involved in the Western import and export trade. Now in Table XV, this same kind of Chinese still predominates. Nevertheless quite

117

TABLE XIV

CHINESE WHO WERE MEMBERS OF THE CHINESE ADVISORY BOARD FOR TEN YEARS OR MORE BETWEEN 1890 AND 1930

Name and Birthplace	Education	Occupation	Relevant Comments
Tan Jiak Kim Singapore	private English education	shipping, commission business	grandson of Malacca Chinese, Tan Kim Seng
Lee Cheng Yan Malacca	not known	commission agent and general trader	
Seah Liang Seah Singapore	secondary English education	gambier and pepper, general trader in cotton and tea	son of Seah Eu Chin
Tan Yong Siak China	not known	cloth merchant, commission agent, dealer in general produce and Siamese rice	
Lim Boon Keng Singapore	secondary and tertiary English education	rubber, tin, insurance, and banking business	
Go Sin Kho Straits-born	not known	merchant	
Lim Ho Pua China	not known	shipping business	wife, a grand-daughter of Malacca Chinese, Kiong Kong Tuan
Leong Mann Sau China	secondary English education	timber business	
Tchan Chun Fook Straits-born (Penang)	secondary English education	managed business of Whampoa and Co.	nephew of Whampoa
Wee Kim Yam Singapore	not known	gambier and pepper business	son of Malacca Chinese, Wee Ah Hood
Yow Ngan Pan Singapore	secondary English education	shipping and banking business	father, a good friend of Whampoa
Liau Chia Heng China	not known	rubber, gambier and pepper, banking, and cloth business	
Low Cheang Yee Singapore	secondary English education	gutta percha and other products	

TABLE XV

CHINESE WHO WERE MEMBERS OF THE CHINESE ADVISORY BOARD FOR SEVEN YEARS OR MORE BETWEEN 1930 AND 1940

Name and Birthplace	Education	Occupation	Relevant Comments
See Teong Wah Singapore	secondary English education	shipping, and banking business	descended from Malacca Chinese
Lim Peng Siang China	secondary English education	banking, shipping, rice, oil mill, cement, and coconut business	descended from Malacca Chinese
Tan Sian Cheng China	not known	banking business	
Seah Eng Tong Singapore	secondary English education	family involved in pineapple, rubber, and preserved fruit	grandson of Seah Eu Chin
Tan Khye Kok not known	not known	merchant	He was involved in the early 1920s in the challenge against the leadership of the Chambers by a Malacca Chinese, See Teong Wah.
Cheong Kee Sun not known	not known	oil mill business	
Ng Sen Choy Straits-born (Penang)	secondary English education	cloth, medicinal products business	
Lee Wee Nam China	some formal Chinese education	banking, remittance, and import and export business	
Lim Boon Thim China	some formal Chinese education	pawnshop business	
Yeo Chang Boon China	some formal Chinese education	cloth and local produce merchant	
Yeung Yip Lim China	some formal Chinese education	contractor and in the sawmill business	

a few members exhibited more 'Chinese' characteristics, such as birth in China and a Chinese education. Many of them were also involved in nationally-based businesses. Thus the presence of the latter group in some numbers on the Board after the 1930s would indicate that the British did not have it entirely their own way after the Depression. It is also worthy of mention that, despite the fact that the Malacca Chinese had lost ground in the economy well before 1930 (see the Chambers' list in Chapter V) they were still retained by the British as advisers on Chinese matters. Presumably, the more 'Chinese' merchants could not make an impact on the Board before the 1930s because of their then great dependence on the Western-dominated economy.

Thus, as in the two previous cases of fundamental changes in the international economy, during free trade and colonialism, the Depression of the 1920s and 1930s also had a profound impact on the nature of the Chinese mercantile class and provided the impetus for many of their members to free themselves from the Western-dominated economy. It is beyond the scope of this book to examine the extent of this independence. But one thing is clear: there can be no doubt that the international economy had a decisive influence on the nature of the Chinese mercantile class in Singapore in the period under review.

1. The most famous example is Tan Kah Kee.

BIBLIOGRAPHY

Documents, Correspondence, etc.

Letters: Letters from the missionary, J. Stronach, to the London Missionary Society, found in London Missionary Society Headquarters, London, May 14, August 22, 23 and 27, 1839; November 26, 1840; September 24 and October 21, 1841.

Parliamentary Papers: British Parliamentary Papers (Command Paper 1686), 1852-3. 'Correspondence with the Superintendent of British trade in China under the subject of emigration from that country.'

Records: *Pelbagai Rekod* (Miscellaneous Records) in The State Archives in Johore, No. S. 13.

Reports: Report of the United States Consul in Singapore found in University of Singapore Library, Singapore.

CONCERNING THE STRAITS SETTLEMENTS

Records of the Government of the Straits Settlements (preserved in the National Library, Singapore).

Indian Administration

    Series A—Penang, Singapore, and Malacca Consultations, 1806-30.

        M—Singapore: Letters to and from Bengal, 1823-61

        N—Singapore: Resident's Diary, 1827-9

        Q—Singapore: Miscellaneous, 1826-73

        Z—Governor's Letters to Singapore, 1827-64

        BB—Singapore: Miscellaneous In, 1823-66

        CC—Singapore: Miscellaneous Out, 1825-67

Records of the Government of India relating to the Straits Settlements

Records of the East India Company and the India Office (preserved in the India Office Library, London)

East India Company

    Secret Correspondence, 1819-67

    Board's Drafts of Secret Letters and Dispatches to India

Secret Letters received from Bengal
Enclosures to Secret Letters received from Bengal and India
Colonial Office Records (preserved at the Public Record Office, London)
Co 273 Series. Straits Settlements, Original Correspondence

OTHERS

Annual Report of the Chinese Protectorate in Singapore
Straits Settlements Blue Book
Straits Settlements Census
Straits Settlements Civil Service Lists
Straits Settlements Gazette

Newspapers and Directories

Colonial Directory, Straits Settlements
Malacca Weekly Chronicle, Malacca
Singapore Chronicle, Singapore
Singapore Daily Times, Singapore
Singapore Free Press, Singapore
Straits Guardian, Singapore
Straits Times, Singapore
Straits Directory
Singapore and Malayan Directory

Periodicals, Journals, Encyclopaedias, etc.

Asian Affairs (Tokyo)
Asian Studies (Quezon City)
Asiatic Journal and Monthly Miscellany (London)
China Quarterly (London)
Chinese Repository (Canton)
Comparative Studies in Society and History (The Hague)
Encyclopaedie Van Nederlandsch-Indie (Leiden)
Frasers Magazine (London)
Journal of Asian Studies (Ann Arbor)
Journal of the Indian Archipelago and East Asia (Singapore)
Journal of Oriental Studies (Hong Kong)
Journal of the Royal Asiatic Society, Malayan Branch and Straits Branch (Singapore)
Journal of Southeast Asian History (Singapore)

Journal of the South Seas Society (Singapore)
Malayan Journal of Tropical Geography (Singapore)
Modern Asian Studies (Cambridge)
Penang Register and Monthly Miscellaneous (Penang)
Social and Economic Studies (Jamaica)
Straits Chinese Magazine (Singapore)
YULE, SIR HENRY, AND A. C. BURNELL, *Hobson-Jobson; a glossary of colloquial Anglo-Indian words and phrases and of kindred terms, etymological, historical, geographical and discussive*, 2nd edition (New Delhi, Munshiram Manoharlal, 1968).

Books

ALLEN, G., AND DONNITHORNE, A., *Western Enterprise in Malaya and Indonesia, A Study in Economic Development* (New York, Macmillan, 1957).

AWBERRY, S. S., AND DALLEY, F. W., *Labour and Trade Union Organization in the Federation of Malaya* (Kuala Lumpur, Government Press, 1948).

BLYTHE, W., *The Impact of Chinese Secret Societies in Malaya, A Historical Study* (London, Oxford University Press, 1969).

BODELSEN, C. A., *Studies in Mid-Victorian Imperialism* (London, Heinemann, 1960).

BOWRING, J., *The Kingdom and People of Siam*, Vol. 1 (London, Parker and Son, 1857).

BUCKLEY, C. B., *An Anecdotal History of Singapore in Old Times* (Singapore, University of Malaya Press, 1965 reprint).

CAMERON, J., *Our Tropical Possessions in Malayan India, being a descriptive account of Singapore, Penang, Province Wellesley, and Malacca: their peoples, products, commerce and government* (London, Smith, Elder and Co., 1865).

CHEN MONG HOCK, *The Early Chinese Newspapers of Singapore, 1881-1902* (Singapore, University of Malaya Press, 1967).

CHEN TA, *Chinese Migrations with Special Reference to Labor Conditions* (Taipeh, Cheng-Wen Publishing Co., 1967).

——— *Emigrant Communities in South China; a study of overseas migration and its influence on standards of living and social change* (New York, Secretariat, Institute of Pacific Relations, 1940).

CHESNEAUX, J., *Secret Societies in China in the Nineteenth and Twentieth Centuries*, translated by Gillian Nettle (Hong Kong,

Heinemann Educational Books Ltd., 1971).

——— (ed.), *Popular Movements and Secret Societies in China 1840-1950* (Stanford, Stanford University Press, 1972).

COMBER, L., *Chinese Secret Societies in Malaya, a Survey of the Triad Society from 1800 to 1900* (New York, Locust Valley, 1959).

——— *Chinese Temples in Singapore* (Singapore, Eastern Universities Press, 1958).

COWAN, C. D., *Nineteenth Century Malaya, the Origins of British Control* (London, Oxford University Press, 1961).

CRAWFURD, J., *History of the Indian Archipelago containing an account of the manners, arts, languages, religions, institutions, and commerce of its inhabitants* (Edinburgh, A. Constable and Co., 1820).

DAVIDSON, G. F., *Trade and Travel in the Far East*, or *Recollections of twenty-one years passed in Java, Singapore, Australia, and China* (London, Madden and Malcolm, 1846).

EARL, G. W., *The Eastern Seas, or voyages and adventures in the Indian Archipelago in 1832-33-34, comprising a tour of Java, visits to Borneo, the Malay peninsula, etc., also an account of the present state of Singapore* (London, Allen and Co., 1837).

ELLIOTT, J. A., *Chinese Spirit-medium Cults in Singapore* (London, London School of Economics, 1955).

FEI HSIAO-TUNG, *The Chinese Gentry/Essays in Rural-Urban Relations*, revised and edited by M. P. Redfield (Chicago, Chicago University Press, 1968).

FREEDMAN, M., *Chinese Family and Marriage in Singapore* (London, H. M. Stationery Office, 1957).

FURNIVALL, J. S., *Netherlands India* (Cambridge, Cambridge University Press, 1967 reprint).

GREENBERG, M., *British Trade and the Opening of China, 1800-42* (Cambridge, Cambridge University Press, 1951).

HAN SUYIN, *The Crippled Tree* (New York, Putnam, 1965).

HOBSBAWM, E., *Primitive Rebels, Studies in archaic forms of social movement in the 19th and 20th centuries* (New York, Norton and Co., 1965).

JACKSON, J., *Planters and Speculators, Chinese and European agricultural enterprise in Malaya 1786-1921* (Singapore, University of Malaya Press, 1968).

KHOO KAY KIM, *The Western Malay States 1850-1873, the effects of commercial development on Malay politics* (Kuala Lumpur, Oxford University Press, 1972).

KUHN, P., *Rebellion and its enemies in late imperial China: militarization and social structures 1796-1864* (Harvard, Harvard University Press, 1970).

MCNAIR, J. F. A., *Prisoners their own Warders* (London, A. Constable, 1899).

MAKEPEACE, W., BROOKE, G. E. AND BRADDELL, R. ST. J. (eds.), *One Hundred Years of Singapore, being some account of the capital of the Straits Settlements from its foundation by Sir Stamford Raffles on the 6th February 1819 to the 6th February 1919* (London, John Murray, 1921).

MILLS, L. A., *British Malaya 1826-67* (Kuala Lumpur, Oxford University Press, 1966 reprint).

MOOR, J. H., *Notices of Indian Archipelago and Adjacent Countries* (Singapore, 1837).

MOORE, D., *The First 150 Years of Singapore* (Singapore, Donald Moore Press, 1969).

MOORE, E. BARRINGTON, *Social Origins of Dictatorship and Democracy, Lord and Peasant in the making of the Modern World* (Boston, Beacon Press, 1966).

NEWBOLD, T. J., *British Settlements in the Straits of Malacca*, Vol. 1 (London, John Murray, 1839).

NEWELL, W. H., *Treacherous River: A study of rural Chinese in North Malaya* (Kuala Lumpur, University of Malaya Press, 1962).

PARKINSON, C. N., *British Intervention in Malaya, 1867-1877* (Singapore, University of Malaya Press, 1960).

PEARSON, H. F., *People of Early Singapore* (London, University of London Press, 1955).

PURCELL, V., *The Chinese in Southeast Asia* (London, Oxford University Press, 1964, 2nd edition).

PYE, L., *Guerilla Communism in Malaya, its Social and Political Meaning* (Princeton, Princeton University Press, 1956).

READ, W. H., *Play and Politics; recollections of Malaya by an old resident* (London, Darto and Co., 1901).

SAW SWEE HOCK, *Singapore Population in Transition* (Philadelphia, University of Pennsylvania Press, 1970).

SCHLEGEL, G., *Thian Ti Hwui, the Hung League or Heaven and Earth League* (Detroit, College Park, 1866).

SIM, V., *Biographies of Prominent Chinese in Singapore* (Singapore, Nan Kok Publications Co., 1950).

SIMONIYA, N. A., *Overseas Chinese in Southeast Asia—a Russian study* (Ithaca, Cornell University Press, 1961).

SKINNER, G. W., *Chinese Society in Thailand, an Analytical History* (Ithaca, Cornell University Press, 1957).

———— *Leadership and Power in the Chinese Community of Thailand* (Ithaca, Cornell University Press, 1958).

SONG ONG SIANG, *One Hundred Years of the Chinese in Singapore* (Singapore, University of Malaya Press, 1967 reprint).

STENSON, M., *Industrial Conflict in Malaya; Prelude to the Communist Revolt of 1948* (London, Oxford University Press, 1970).

TILMAN, R. O. (ed.), *Man, State and Society in Contemporary Southeast Asia* (New York, Praeger, 1969).

TUNG TSU CHU, *Local Government in China under the Ching* (Stanford, Stanford University Press, 1969).

TURNBULL, C. M., *The Straits Settlements 1826-67, Indian Presidency to Crown Colony* (London, The Athlone Press, 1972).

UCHIDA, N., *The Overseas Chinese; a bibliographical essay based on the resources of the Hoover Institution* (Stanford, Stanford University Press, 1959).

VAUGHAN, J. D., *Manners and Customs of the Chinese in the Straits Settlements* (Singapore, Mission Press, 1879).

WALLACE, A. R., *The Malay Archipelago, the Land of the Orang Utan, and the Bird of Paradise* (New York, Harper and Brothers, 1869).

WANG GUNGWU, *A Short History of the Nanyang Chinese* (Singapore, Eastern Universities Press, 1959).

WARD, J.S., AND STIRLING, W. G., *The Hung Society or the Society of Heaven and Earth, 1925-26* (London, Baskerville Press, 1925).

WEE MON CHENG, *The Future of the Overseas Chinese in Southeast Asia: as viewed from the economic angle, and other articles on economic topics* (Singapore, University Education Press, 1972).

WICKBERG, E., *The Chinese in Philippine Life 1850-1898* (New Haven, Yale University Press, 1965).

WILLMOTT, W., *The Political Structure of the Chinese Community in Cambodia* (London, The Athlone Press, 1970).

WONG, C. S., *A Gallery of Chinese Kapitans* (Singapore, Ministry of Culture, 1963).

WRIGHT, A., AND CARTWRIGHT, H. A. (eds.), *Twentieth Century Impressions of British Malaya: its history, people, commerce, industries and resources* (London, Lloyd's Greater Britain Publishing Co. Ltd., 1908).

———— *Twentieth Century Impressions of Hong Kong, Shanghai, and other Treaty Ports of China: their history, people, commerce, industries, and resources* (London, Lloyd's Greater Britain Publishing Co. Ltd., 1908).

WYNNE, MERVYN LLEWELLYN, *Triad and Tabut—A Survey of the Origin and Diffusion of Chinese and Mohammedan Secret Societies in the Malay Peninsula A.D. 1800-1935* (Singapore, Government Printing Office, 1957).

Monographs, Data Papers, etc.

JACKSON, R. N., *Immigrant Labour and the Development of Malaya, 1786-1920* (Kuala Lumpur, Government Press, 1961).

MORSE, H. B., *The Gilds of China with an account of the Gild Merchant or Co-Hong of Canton* (Shanghai, Kelly and Walsh, 1932).

SARDESAI, D. R., *Trade and Empire in Malaya and Singapore 1869-1874* (Athens, Ohio University Press, 1970).

STENSON, M., *Repression and revolt: the origins of the 1948 Communist insurrection in Malaya and Singapore* (Athens, Ohio University Press, 1969).

T'IEN JU-KANG, *The Chinese in Sarawak, a Study of Social Structure* (London, London School of Economics and Political Science, 1953).

WONG LIN KEN, *The Trade of Singapore, 1819-1869*, found in *Journal of Royal Asiatic Society* (Malayan Branch), Vol. XXXIII, No. 4, (1960).

Articles

ABDULLAH BIN ABDUL KADIR, MUNSHI, 'Concerning the Tan Tae Hoey in Singapore', trans. by T. Braddell, *Journal of the Indian Archipelago*, VI (1852).

BARTLEY, W., 'Population of Singapore in 1819', *Journal of Royal Asiatic Society (Malayan Branch)*, XI, No. 2 (1933).

BRADDELL, T., 'Gambling and Smoking in the Straits of Malacca', *Journal of the Indian Archipelago*, n.s.i. (1857).

———— 'Notes on the Chinese in the Straits', *Journal of the Indian Archipelago*, IX (1855).

———— 'Notices of Singapore', *Journal of the Indian Archipelago*, VII (1853), VIII (1854), IX (1855).

FIELDHOUSE, D. K., 'Imperialism: an Historiographical Revision',

The Economic History Review, Second Series XIV, No. 2 (1961).

EE, J., 'Chinese Migration to Singapore, 1896-1941', *Journal of Southeast Asian History*, II (1961).

FREEDMAN, M., 'Immigrants and Associations: Chinese in 19th-Century Singapore', *Comparative Studies in Society and History*, III (October 1960).

———— 'Overseas Chinese Associations: a Comment', *Society and History*, III (1961).

———— 'Chinese Marriage and Family in Early Singapore', *Journal of Southeast Asian History* (1962).

FRIED, M., 'Clans and Lineages: how to tell them apart and why—with special reference to Chinese Society', in *An Anthology by the Academica Sinica on Ethnological Research*, Spring, 1970, Taiwan.

GALLAGHER, J. AND ROBINSON, R., 'The Imperialism of Free Trade', *The Economic History Review*, Vol. VI, No. 1 (August 1953).

LITTLE, R., 'On the Habitual Use of Opium in Singapore', 'Modes of Using Opium', 'Provisions of the Opium Regulations for Singapore and Hong Kong', *Journal of the Indian Archipelago*, II (1848).

———— 'Opium Smoking', *Journal of the Indian Archipelago*, III (1849).

NEWBOLD, LT. AND WILSON, MAJOR-GENERAL, 'The Chinese Secret Societies of the Tien Ti-huih', *Journal of Royal Asiatic Society (Northern Ireland and England)*, Vol. VI (1841).

NG SIEW YOONG, 'The Chinese Protectorate in Singapore, 1877-1900', *Journal of Southeast Asian History*, II, No. 1 (March 1961).

PICKERING, W. A., 'The Chinese in the Straits of Malacca', *Frasers Magazine* (October 1876).

———— 'Chinese Secret Societies', *Journal of Royal Asiatic Society (Straits Branch)*, I and III (1878-9).

SEAH EU CHIN, 'The Chinese in Singapore', *Journal of the Indian Archipelago*, II (1848).

SHELLABEAR, R. G., 'Baba Malay: an introduction to the language of the Straits Chinese', *Journal of Royal Asiatic Society (Malayan Branch)*, LXV (December 1913).

SKINNER, G. W., 'Change and Persistence in Chinese Culture Overseas; a comparison of Thailand and Java', *Journal of South Seas Society*, XVI (1960).

A Straits Chinese, 'Local Chinese Social Organizations', *The Straits Chinese Magazine*, III (1899).

TAN EE LEONG, 'Chinese Banks incorporated in Singapore and the Federation of Malaya', *Journal of Royal Asiatic Society* (*Malayan Branch*), Vol. 26, Part 1 (July 1953).

TAN TEK SOON, 'Chinese Local Trade', *The Straits Chinese Magazine*, VI (1902).

THIO, E., 'The Singapore Chinese Protectorate: events and conditions leading to its establishment 1823-77', *Journal of South Seas Society*, XVI (1960).

THOMSON, J., 'Agricultural labourers', in 'General report of the Residency of Singapore, drawn up principally with a view of illustrating the agricultural statistics', *Journal of the Indian Archipelago*, III (1849).

TOPLEY, M., 'The emergence and social functions of Chinese religious associations in Singapore', *Comparative Studies in Society and History*, III (1961).

TURNBULL, C. M., 'Gambier and Pepper Trade in Johore in the Nineteenth Century', *Journal of South Seas Society*, XV, Part 1 (1959).

WARD, B., 'A Hakka Kongsi in Borneo', *Journal of Oriental Studies*, I (1954).

WILLIAMS, L., 'Chinese leadership in early Singapore', *Asian Studies*, Vol. 2, Part 2 (August 1964).

YEN CHING HWANG, 'Ching's sale of honours and the Chinese leadership in Singapore and Malaya (1877-1912)', *Journal of Southeast Asian Studies* (September 1970).

YONG CHING FATT, 'A preliminary study of Chinese leadership in Singapore 1900-41', *Journal of Southeast Asian History* (September 1968).

Unpublished Theses

BOGAARS, G., 'The Suez Canal and the Singapore Trade', B. A. academic exercise, University of Malaya, Singapore, 1951.

CHIA, GRACE, BENG IMM, 'Asian Members of the Straits Settlements Legislative Council (1908-41)', B. A. academic exercise, University of Singapore, 1960.

FREEDMAN, M., 'Kinship, Local Organization and Migration; a study in social realignment among Chinese overseas', Ph.D. Thesis, University of London, 1956.

FUNG, AGNES, LI-NING, 'Growth of Settlements in Rural Singapore, 1819-1957', B. A. academic exercise, University of Singapore, 1961-2.

GOH PENG WEE, 'A Study of the Kinship Relations of Some Teochew (Chaochow) Nuclear Families in Singapore', Diploma in Social Studies Thesis, University of Malaya (Singapore), 1960.

LEE AH-CHAI, 'Policies and Politics in Chinese Schools in the Straits Settlements and the Federated Malay States, 1786-1941', M. A. Thesis, University of Malaya (Singapore), 1957.

LOH WEN FONG, 'Singapore Agency Houses 1819-1900', B. A. academic exercise, University of Malaya (Singapore), 1958.

WEN CHUNG CHI, '19th Century Imperial Chinese Consulate in Straits Settlements: Origins and Development', M. A. Thesis, University of Singapore.

YEN CHING HWANG, 'Chinese Revolutionary Movement in Malaya', Ph.D. Thesis, Australian National University (Canberra), 1970.

IN CHINESE

CHANG LI-CH'IEN (張禮千), *Ma-lu-chia shih* 馬六甲史 (*A History of Malacca.*) Singapore, 1941.

CH'EN YU-SUNG (TAN YOEK SEONG) AND CH'EN CHING HO (陳育崧, 陳荊和), *Hsin-chia-po hua-wen pei-ming chi-lu* 新加坡華文碑銘集錄 (*Collection of Chinese Inscriptions in Singapore.*) Hongkong, 1973.

CHOU HAN-JEN (周漢人), *Nan-yang hua-chiao jen-wu-chih yu ch'iao-chou ko hsien yen ke shih* 南洋潮僑人物誌與潮州各縣沿革史 (*Biographies of Overseas Teochew Leaders with history of Teochew districts.*) Singapore, 1958.

HO PING-TI (何炳棣), *Chung-kuo hui-kuan shih-lun* 中國會館史論 (*On the history of landsmannschaften in China.*) Taipei, 1966.

LEE I-CHI (LEE YIK CHEE) (李奕志), 'Hsin-chia-po hua-wen ssu-hui-tang chin hsi' *Tung-nan-ya yen-chiu* '新加坡華人私會黨今昔' 東南亞研究 ('The Past and Present Days of Chinese Secret Societies in Singapore') *Journal of Southeast Asian Researches*, Volume 7, Singapore, 1971.

LI CHUNG-CHIO (李鍾珏), *Hsin-chia-po feng-t'u-chi* 新加坡風土記 (*A Description of Singapore.*) Singapore, 1947.

LIN PO-AI and others (林博愛等), *Nan-yang ming-jen chi-chuan* 南洋名人集傳 (*A Collection of Famous Men in South East Asia.*) Penang, 1922.

P'AN HSING-NUNG (潘醒農), *Ma-la-ya ch'ao-ch'iao t'ung-chien* 馬來亞潮僑通鑑 (*The Teochews in Malaya.*) Singapore, 1950.

SU HSIAO-HSIEN (蘇孝先), *Chang-chou shih-shu lu-hsing t'ung-*

hsiang-lu 漳州十屬旅星同鄉錄 (*Chronicles of the Residents of Changchou.*) Singapore, 1950.

SUNG CHO-YING (宋卓英), *Hsien-tai tung-nan-ya ch'eng-kung-jen-wu-chih* 現代東南亞成功人物誌 (*The Successful Men of Southeast Asia.*) Singapore, 1968.

SUNG CHE-MEI (宋哲美), *Hsing-ma jen-wu-chih* 星馬人物誌 (*Who's who in Malaya and Singapore.*) Hongkong, 1969.

T'IEN JU-KANG (田汝康), *17-19 shih-chi chung-kuo fan-ch'uan tsai tung-nan-ya chou* 17-19 世紀中國帆船在東南亞洲 (*Seventeenth to Nineteenth Century Chinese Junk Trade in South-East Asia.*) Shanghai, 1957.

Publications of Clans, Dialect Groups, Territorial Associations and Others

Hsin-chia-po chung-hua-tsung-shang-hui ta hsia lo ch'eng chi-nien-kan 新加坡中華總商會大廈落成紀念刊 (*Souvenir of the Opening Ceremony of the Newly Completed Singapore Chinese Chamber of Commerce Building.*) Singapore, 1964.

Hsin-chia-po chung-hua tsung-shang-hui ch'ing chu tsuan hsi chi-nien-t'e-kan 新加坡中華總商會慶祝鑽禧紀念特刊. (*The Souvenir of the Sixtieth Anniversary of the Singapore Chinese Chamber of Commerce.*) Singapore, 1966.

Hsin-chia-po chung-hua-tsung-shang-hui ch'ing-chi-yueh-pao 新加坡中華總商會經濟月報 (*Economic Monthly: Journal of the Singapore Chinese Chamber of Commerce.*) Singapore.

Hsin-chia-po ch'a-yang-hui-kuan I pai chou nien chi-nien-t'e-kan 新加坡茶陽會館一百週年紀念特刊 (*Special Publication of the 100th Anniversary Celebration of the Singapore Ch'a-yang hui-kuan.*) Singapore, 1958.

Hsin-chia-po ch'iao-chou-pa-I-hui-kuan ssu shih chou chi-nien 新加坡潮州八邑會館四十週年紀念 (*Publication of the Fortieth Anniversary Celebration of the Ch'iao-chou hui-kuan.*) Singapore, 1969.

Hsin-chia-po ning-yang-hui-kuan I pai san shih chou nien chi-nien t'e-kan 新加坡寧陽會館一百三十週年紀念特刊 (*Special Publication of the 130th Anniversary Celebration of the Singapore Ning-yang-hui-kuan.*) Singapore, 1952.

Hsing-chou ying-ho-hui-kuan I pai ssu shih chou nien chi-nien t'e-kan 星洲應和會館一百四十一週年紀念特刊 (*Special Publication of the 140th Anniversary Celebration of the Singapore Ying-ho-hui-*

kuan.) Singapore, 1965.

Hsing-chou shih-nien, Hsing-chou-yueh-pao shih-chou-nien chi-nien t'e-kan 星洲十年，星洲日報十週年紀念特刊 (*Ten Years of Singapore, Special Tenth Anniversary Publication of the Hsing-chou-yueh-pao.*) Singapore, 1940.

Lung-hsi-li-shih chi-nien t'e-kan 隴西李氏紀念特刊 (*Special Commemorative Publication of the Lung-hsi-li-shih clan.*)

Nan-an-hui-kuan san shih chou-nien chi-nien t'e-kan 南安會館三十週年紀念特刊 (*Special Publication of the Thirtieth Anniversary Celebration of the Singapore Nan-an-hui-kuan.*) Singapore, 1949.

Nan-shun-hui-kuan ching tseng 南順會館敬贈 (*Publication of the Nan-shun-hui-kuan.*) Singapore, 1964.

Nan-yang nien-chien 南洋年鑑 (*Nan-yang Yearbook.*) Singapore, 1951.

Nan-yang k'e-shu-tsung-hui ti san shih wu lu chou-nien chi-nien-kan 南洋客屬總會第三第三十五六週年紀念刊 (*Thirty-fifth and Thirty-sixth Special Commemorative Publication of the Nanyang Khek Community Guild, Singapore.*) Singapore, 1967.

Yang-shih-chia-p'u 楊氏家譜 (*Genealogy of the Yang Clan.*) Kuala Lumpur, 1962.

NEWSPAPERS

Li-pao (*Lat Pau*) Singapore 叻報

Yueh-hsin-pao (*Jit Shin Pao.*) Singapore 日新報

INDEX

ABSCONDING BY CHINESE, 16, 17, 18, 20

Agents, agency houses, 6, 14-15, 16, 17, 18-20

Agriculture, *see* Gambier and pepper society; Land tenure; Plantations

Ahun-Teo, 52

Anderson, Benedict R.O.G., ix, x

Ang Ah Hiang, 53

Ang Kim Cheak, 22

Anglo-Dutch Treaty (1824), 11

Artisans, Chinese, 26, 27, 37, 39, 40

Assimilation of Chinese, 4-8

Aw Boon Haw, 105, 115

Ayun Ko, 52

BANGKOK, 35n, 107

Bangsalls, 72

Banking, 100, 101, 102, 103, 104, 106, 107, 108, 115, 116, 117,118

Bankruptcy law, 17

Barter system, 14, 15

Batavia, 14

Beri-beri, 29

Blythe, W.L., 47

Boey Ah Ghee, 23

Bonham, Superintendent of Police, 51

Borneo, 28

Bowring Treaty (1855), 73, 74

British: free trade era of, ix, 4, 13-27; acquisition of Singapore by (1819), 11, 17; government in India's attitude to Singapore, 3; military intervention in Singapore, 55; relations between Chinese merchants and, 14-15, 37, 54-5, 64, 66, 96-7; riots and, 64, 70, 75; control of Chinese monopolies and shipping by, 73-4, 75, 76; and of remittance business, 64, 75-6; 1857 general strike and, 78-80; political intervention by, ix, 81, 85-97, 113; adviser system, 85; reliance on secret societies by, 89-90; and proscription of secret societies, 90-1, 113; and establishment of friendly societies, 91-3, 95; and Chinese Advisory Board, 91, 96; *see also* Free trade society

British East India Company, 11

Buckley, C.B., 74, 75

Bugis, 27

Building trade/materials, 101, 102, 116

Bukit Timah Road/settlement, *68*, 69-70, 72, 75

CAMBODIA, 5

Canton, British blockade of, 78

Cantonese, 39, 40, *41*, 46, 87, 89, 96, 97n, 105, 106, 107

Chan Koo Chan, 23

Chan Sze Jin, 109

Chang Fei, 48

Chang Pi-shih, 110n

Changchou Association, 60n

Changi Road, 69

Chao-chou prefecture, 76

Cheang Ah Hong, 53

Cheang Hong Lim, 22

Chee Teang Why, 21, 23

Cheong Kee Sun, 118

Chesneaux, Jean, 49

Chia Lek, 22

Chin Yong Kwong, 105, 114